TRAVELS THROUGH PREHISTORIC SPAIN: A GUIDE

TRAVELS THROUGH PREHISTORIC SPAIN

A GUIDE

Jude Brown and Gary Lock

Archaeopress Archaeology

Archaeopress Publishing Ltd
13-14 Market Square
Bicester
Oxfordshire OX26 6AD
United Kingdom

www.archaeopress.com

ISBN 978-1-80583-090-0
ISBN 978-1-80583-091-7 (e-Pdf)

Cover: Tony Buckmaster

Contents

Introduction

This book has been a labour of love. It combines four things which we have enjoyed doing for many years – travelling in our camper van, visiting different areas of Spain, looking at prehistoric monuments and walking within beautiful landscapes. Spain is obviously a big country and it contains thousands of prehistoric monuments – what we present here is just a small sample of those sites, ones that we have visited and enjoyed. In total we present here over two hundred sites, including some museums with collections of prehistoric material, covering many but not all of the autonomous regions of Spain.

Our two criteria for including a site are that firstly it has to be relatively easy to find and that secondly there has to be something interesting to see once you get there. Of course, these are both fairly subjective and some of the sites involve longish walks or even longer drives along dusty unmade tracks and not everyone may be impressed once the end is reached.

[A personal note from Jude – although I totally agree with this being a labour of love, for me it initially began as an opportunity to have relaxing, interesting holidays in Northern Spain. Being married to an obsessive archaeologist with a specialism in prehistory means that this always colours our times abroad and relaxation hardly comes into it! However the beauty of the Spanish landscapes we travelled through and the chance to seek out different prehistoric sites, from wonderful overhangs with paintings and sculptures which were breathtaking to obviously ancient dwellings with intact walls and even a prehistoric sauna, became addictive. The journey to different provinces to find what traces the ancient past had left behind was fun, exciting and rewarding. Days looking for a dot on the map which was never quite where it should be, dusty walks which always seemed to be in the midday sun and then finding what we were looking for, measuring and photographing it and delighting that it was there and we had found it. I urge others to enjoy this kind of journey as much as I can honestly say I have over at least 13 years of exploration. Remember to take your sun screen, your insect repellent, lots of water, a large hat and some good walking shoes, plenty of patience and good humour too. We both needed that at times!]

Road numbers in Spain can be very confusing. Sometimes roads have more than one number and sometimes the numbers change. This is especially true as we started this endeavour in 2010 so some of the information included here may be out of date. Even so, the sites should still be there. We used the Michelin regional maps at 1/250,000 together with our satnav and web searches. Information on the internet is vastly improved since we started this survey and it may be that you don't need the paper maps at all although we still find them useful as a backup. We have attempted to give directions to each monument although sometimes signposting is non-existent or at best minimal so apologies in advance if you don't find what you are looking for. All is not lost however as these monuments usually involve nice walking across some spectacular and lovely landscapes. Over the years we have undergone many wild goose chases convinced that a good site was within reach only to fail to find it.

Generally speaking Spain is very proud of its cultural heritage and provides good access and information. Many towns both large and small have good museums with prehistoric collections although this does vary across the different autonomous regions. Many individual sites, or towns/villages close to them, have interpretation centres run by the local authority which are always worth visiting first to gain information and, sometimes, maps and leaflets describing sites and archaeological trails. We have indicated these in the text where appropriate. For the most detailed presentation of Spanish prehistory the National Archaeological Museum in Madrid is a must see (page 1).

We have not included information about site and museum opening times as these can, and do, change. Current information can be found at local tourist information offices and/or on the internet. As a rough guide we indicate whether a site/museum is restricted access (there are opening hours) or unrestricted access (the site is permanently open).

Chronology and sites

It is useful here to explain prehistoric chronology generally and how that applies to Spain as well as mentioning the main types of sites described for each period. Here we offer a simple outline with pointers to where in the book more detail is presented.

At its simplest level prehistory is 'before writing' although this is more complicated in some places and especially towards the end of the period in Europe due to contact with the Romans and earlier in Spain with the Phoenicians (more on this below). Prehistory is divided into the so-called Three Age System of the Stone, Bronze and Iron Ages reflecting technological changes. This was first suggested in 1836 by the Dane C. J. Thomsen based on his work with the collections in the National Museum in Copenhagen. Since that time the vast amount of new archaeological evidence together with new interpretations have developed detailed sub-divisions of these three periods. The development of scientific dating methods, especially radiocarbon dating since the 1960s, has enabled absolute dates to be established for prehistoric periods.

The Stone Age is subdivided into the Palaeolithic (Old Stone Age), the Mesolithic (Middle Stone Age) and the Neolithic (New Stone Age). The Palaeolithic is an immensely long span of time starting at least 3 million years ago and covers the development of humans and our predecessors from the earliest forms in Africa to modern humans, Homo sapiens sapiens, appearing between 120,000 and 90,000 years ago in Africa and spreading across the globe. Some of the pre-modern forms of the genus Homo were in Spain and by far the best place to experience them is the very impressive Centre for Human Evolution in Burgos and the nearby site of Atapuerca where evidence for them living and dying has been found (page 130).

This long period is subdivided into shorter periods based mainly on the development of stone tools which generally speaking start crude and become more and more finely worked with an ever-increasing range of tool types. Through detailed excavation of sites where Palaeolithic people lived, many in the mouths of caves but not always, there is also increasing evidence of other aspects of ancient life such as the development of diet and food preparation and burial practices, for example as shown in the Serinyà Prehistoric Caves Park, Catalunya (page 188). An intriguing area of research over many decades has concerned the religious beliefs and aesthetic considerations of these people including what we would call art.

Modern humans spread out from Africa and reached Spain at around 38,000 years ago overlapping with Homo sapiens neanderthalensis (Neanderthals) who had been in that part of Europe since about 90,000 years ago. Genetic evidence shows that there was a certain amount of interbreeding between the two subspecies until neanderthals became extinct at about 40,000 years ago. Evidence for the Palaeolithic is offered in many of the museums mentioned below but in terms of visiting sites we are mainly limited to caves and cave art. The north-western coast of Spain, mainly the autonomous regions of País Vasco, Cantabria and Asturias, is one of the main centres for cave art in Europe with many spectacular sites to visit, not least Altamira with its fabulous frieze of coloured bison (page 12).

Palaeolithic cave art reached its zenith in the Magdalenian sub-period, *c.* 17,000 to 13,000 years ago, although there is similar art from the earlier Solutrean period, from 20,000 years ago. In all its forms Palaeolithic art spans a period of just before 30,000 to 10,000 years ago. There are a few examples of other forms of Palaeolithic art and Siega Verde, Castilla y León (page 114) is a good example. Here panels of inscribed animals are on slabs of bedrock along a river valley. Inscribed art also occurs on bones and stones, generally called mobile art, much of which can be seen in museums.

During the Palaeolithic and Mesolithic periods people were hunter gatherers moving around their environment knowing where the herds of animals would be and also the natural fruits and berries to pick. They lived in temporary camps and caves. Following the end of the last glacial period, around 10,000 BC, the climate began to warm and it is around 5,000 BC that we see a major change in lifestyle and archaeological monuments. This is the beginning of the Neolithic period which is characterised by a more sedentary lifestyle, the introduction of pottery making and domesticated animals and cereals, a way of life that spread across Europe from the eastern Mediterranean region. Agriculture and animal husbandry appeared earliest in eastern and southern Spain and spread slowly and irregularly across the rest of Iberia. Here we concentrate on the two forms of Neolithic evidence that are easiest to visit as sites, rock art (arte rupestre and petroglyphs) and megalithic tombs (dolmen), as opposed to the other aspects of Neolithic life which are explained and illustrated in many of the museums mentioned in this book.

Levantine art is known mainly from the south and east of Spain with many examples in Aragón (page 89), it is probably dated to the late Neolithic/early Bronze Age. It differs from Palaeolithic cave art not just in date but in being found within rock overhangs known as rock shelters (abrigos) rather than deep caves and, therefore, originally probably being much more visible. It also differs in its content, whereas cave art is focussed on animals much of the later art depicts humans, both men and women, engaged in a variety of activities providing tantalising glimpses of their lives and society. These include hunting deer and wild goats, collecting honey from hives, dancing and fighting with bows and arrows with details providing information on clothing such as baggy trousers, hairstyles and personal ornaments.

The other major legacy of the Neolithic in terms of what can be seen in today's landscape is megalithic tombs, literally 'large stone' constructions which were various forms of collective burial places starting around 4,000 BC. These are known as 'dolmen' and can be found across Spain, many have been extensively excavated and studied and all museums with a prehistoric collection will display and explain examples of dolmen. Some dolmen are massive and provoke amazement at how the huge stones were moved and placed in position, for example the three near to Antequerra in Andalucía, Dolmen de Viera, Menga and El Romeral (page 166). Others are much smaller but occur in large groups, or cemeteries, such as those in the dramatic landscape around Gorafe, northeast of Granada (page 170). On the island of Menorca a different and unique megalithic tradition can be seen displaying some remarkable structures (page 195).

The first metal-using communities utilised copper before adding it to tin to form bronze, in Spain starting at around 3,200 BC. This period is called the Chalcolithic (Copper Age) and is transitional between the Neolithic and the Bronze Age. During this time we get the arrival from other parts of Europe of the Beaker people named after their distinctive pottery and bringing with them a range of new artefact types and burial practices. Levantine art continued for a while although it changed from showing human figures to being mainly geometric patterns. The big change in the Chalcolithic is evidence for large well organised settlements the prime example of which is Los Millares near Almería (page 175). Here triple walls with entrances and bastions defend a settlement over 2ha in size containing many houses and workshops occupied from about 3,200 BC to 2,300 BC. The tombs in the cemetery contain a range of grave goods suggesting the beginnings of a stratified society with some people being of higher social status than others. These sorts of settlements are not found all over Spain and in many parts the Chalcolithic period is not well represented.

Bronze Age Spain saw different sorts of settlements in different areas and from about 2,000 BC the Chalcolithic settlements were abandoned. We see increasing sophistication in bronze working techniques compared to the relatively simple methods of the earlier period. The much expanded range of tools, weapons and personal decoration as well as pottery types and other domestic items are well represented in many of the museums listed below. There seems to be a growing focus on weapons perhaps suggesting increasing tension and conflict between the emerging tribal groups. In and around Extremadura, for example, there are many Bronze Age stelae, gravestones consisting of a large stone with carvings on it. Many good examples in Badajoz Museum (page 149) show well-armed warriors with helmets, shields, swords and some chariots.

From 800 BC the Mediterranean coast of Spain took a very different developmental trajectory to the areas inland and to the northwest. The arrival of the Phoenicians probably to exploit the mineral wealth of southern Spain established a series of colonies along the coast which became part of extensive trading links to the Greek world further east. From about the 4th century BC Carthaginian traders established colonies and continued the trading until their defeat by the Romans in the Second Punic War in about 200 BC. The Greeks also arrived on the northeast coast of Spain as offshoots of their main city at Marseille although they did establish earlier trading settlements further west. The indigenous Bronze Age people adopted and adapted these new cultural values and opportunities to create a vibrant and exciting culture of their own becoming known as the Iberians. From about 550 BC large Iberian cities were thriving especially along the coast of Andalucía and many of their very rich possessions and ways of life and death can be seen in the important display at the Archaeological Museum in Madrid. Different forms of early writing were in use during these times so these cultures were not prehistoric and, therefore, are not covered in this book.

Of more interest here are the developments to the north and west, the area of the so-called Celtiberians who were influenced by late Bronze Age and Iron Age cultures in central non-

Mediterranean Europe and who remained prehistoric until the arrival of the Romans. These people were organised into many different tribal groups and territories, some living in small farms and villages while others built large, centralised settlements usually called castros. These impressive sites are surrounded by massive stone-built ramparts enclosing stone roundhouses and other buildings. Around Navia in western Asturias, the land of the *Astures*, there are some good examples to visit (page 32), many of which have been excavated such as Coaña and particularly Chao Samartín with its excellent onsite museum. Some of these sites were first constructed in the late Bronze Age but their main period of use is the Iron Age from about 700 BC. In this area many were taken over by the Romans who were exploiting the local gold deposits so that changes in house design can be seen within the castros. One interesting feature within many of these castros are the so-called saunas possibly used for ritual cleansing. The material culture of these Iron Age people was rich and varied as can be seen in many museums, a very good one being the archaeological museum in Oviedo (page 25).

Another area of Iron Age occupation that we cover in some detail is around Ávila in Castilla y León where a series of large castros can be visited (page 120). Here we are in the land of the *Vettones* and sites such as Las Cogotas and Ulaca, some with interpretation centres, give a detailed picture of how these people lived. One interesting aspect of the *Vettones* is their use of the enigmatic verracos, large carved stone bulls and boars, see the particularly impressive group at Guisando (page 126).

It took the Roman legions nearly 200 years to completely subjugate Spain with the northern and western mountainous regions causing them particular problems. A key battle was the siege and eventual defeat of the Celtiberian town of Numancia, Castilla y León (page 133), in 133 BC. The culmination of the Cantabrian wars and the final taking of Asturias in 19 BC saw the end of prehistoric Spain although some aspects of life such as houses, farming and material culture must have continued for a while for many people especially those in more rural areas.

Acknowledgements

Many thanks to Fernando Rodriguez del Cueto and Ángel Villa Valdés for being such good hosts and for their insights and help with the castros of Asturias. Also to César González-Pérez for help with various sites in Galicia. Simon and Barbara Maddison also helped with some sites in southern Galicia, much appreciated. Ade Boulter was a great companion around the caves of the northwest. Interesting conversations were had with Sara Fairen about Levantine Art who also expertly edited the text checking especially for accents and Spanish spellings. Thanks to Ian Ralston for the photographs of sites in Asturias. Many thanks and love also to Sarah and Tony for drawing the maps and the front cover.

Map Locations

Chapter 1
Madrid

The National Archaeological Museum

Calle de Serrano, 13
Restricted access

There is obviously much to see and enjoy in Madrid but one of the delights for anyone interested in prehistory must be this tremendous museum. It was founded in 1867 by Royal Decree of Queen Isabella II and opened in its present location, the neo-classical Palace of the National Library and Museums, in 1892. A complete remodelling and refurbishment of the 19th century building saw the museum being closed for the eight years prior to 2014 when it re-opened. Despite the autonomous regions of Spain having their own museums and claiming their own cultural heritage this national museum still has a collection which spans the country in considerable detail and presents material culture from the Palaeolithic period through to the middle ages.

One of the great strengths of this museum is not just the objects on display but the social and cultural backgrounds of the objects explained through traditional exhibits and through videos and interactive displays. Many of these are in English as well as Spanish. With so much to explore all we can do here is highlight some of our favourite items.

At the entrance don't miss the underground replica of the Cantabrian cave of Altamira (see page 12). Using photogrammetry, the cave is an exact mould of the chamber's shape showing how the polychrome images of animals, especially bison, and hands are located to give an impression of three dimensionality and movement. Other decorated caves have produced a wealth of art engraved on portable objects, many of which are on display here.

Figure 1.1. An engraved deer on a scapulae from Cueva de Castillo, Cantabria (© The National Archaeological Museum, Madrid)

Figure 1.2. A late Bronze Age stela from Extremadura (© The National Archaeological Museum, Madrid)

When inside the museum there is a good display explaining the importance of archaeology and detailing the chronological periods. The Palaeolithic displays give way to the Neolithic and Copper Ages where a highlight must be the remarkable site of Los Millares near Almería (see page 175). This huge site of 2 hectares was occupied between 3,200 and 2,300 BC by up to 1,000 people who constructed massive surrounding stone walls, many houses and tombs. One highlight of the late Bronze Age is the carved gravestones, stelae, which show warriors and their weapons as well as the actual weapons themselves.

The Iron Age section has much information about castros (hillforts) of the north-western provinces (see page 32) which are mainly prehistoric although many were continued into the Roman period. Highlights of the associated material culture must be the many fabulous golden neck torcs and the display of verracos, monumental stone carvings of boar and bulls (see page 126).

Although not strictly prehistory, the protohistoric galleries on the first-floor display some truly remarkable objects (see the map of pre-Roman peoples 5th-1st centuries BC to understand the different cultural groups). One highlight is the display on women in Iberian society, the pre-Roman coastal culture of Andalucia. Foremost is the iconic Dama de Elche discovered in 1897 and dating to the 4th century BC, showing Greek influences and originally coloured by

Figure 1.3. A late Bronze Age sword from Guadalajara (© The National Archaeological Museum, Madrid)

Figure 1.4. An Iron Age gold neck torc from Extremadura (© The National Archaeological Museum, Madrid)

painting. The many other female representations are mainly just heads although the Dama de Baza is a fully seated figure showing wonderful details of costume and jewellery including massive earrings.

Cave Art in Northern Spain
N
W
E
S
SANTANDER
GIJÓN
RIBADESELLA
SAN SEBASTIAN
(M)
OVIEDO (M)
(P) ASTURIAS
BILBAO (M)
FRANCE
CANTABRIA
PAIS VASCO
NAVARRA
CASTILLA Y LEON
Dolmen
Rock Art
Cave Paintings
(M) Museum
(I) Interpretation Centre
(P) Prehistoric Park

Chapter 2

Cave art in north-western Spain: País Vasco, Cantabria and Asturias

Palaeolithic cave art

In 1985 the cave of Altamira was made a World Heritage site and since then another 17 in this area of northern Spain have been added due to the exceptional quality of the Palaeolithic art found within them. Homo sapiens arrived here around 35,000 years ago and lived with the last of the Neanderthals for a while. From 30,000 to 25,000 years ago we can see the beginnings of a distinctive Upper Palaeolithic culture with the introduction of bone and antler projectile points and a range of new flint tools and weapons. As part of this development we get the introduction of art, both on artefacts and through the decoration of cave walls. With the end of the last Ice Age at around 18,000 years ago cave art flourished and reached its height during the Magdalenian period, 17,000 to 13,000 years ago, with many of the main panels of art in a range of caves showing a great variety of motifs and techniques. The use of colour, the combination of engraving and painting, the use of rock forms to produce 3D effects and the realistic detail of large and small animals all make this art not only beautiful to see but provoking to think about. The subsequent warming of the climate caused profound changes in the lifestyles of people and a decline in cave art, the latest being around 11,000 years ago.

Not all the 18 caves are open to the public, here we describe the main ones that are, starting from east to west: between San Sebastián and Bilbao; Santander to Ribadesella and around Oviedo. There are museums in the major cities with displays that cover the Palaeolithic period as well as other periods of prehistory, namely San Sebastián, Bilbao, Santander and Oviedo. If you only want to visit one we would recommend the tremendous new museum in Santander (see below). If you are approaching this area from the west then the Prehistoric Park at Teverga, 30km southwest of Oviedo, is a must.

Note

To visit some of the less popular caves described here it is necessary to book in advance as they do not have ticket offices or guides on site and they all have fences to stop entry. It can be difficult and frustrating trying to find out where to book. We recommend you ask when visiting some of the larger caves that have ticket offices and/or interpretation centres on site. It is also worth asking at local Tourist Information Offices. Searching the internet can also help, all three of the Autonomous Regions covered here, País Vasco, Cantabria and Asturias, have tourist websites although they won't include the lesser well-known caves. You can only enter many of the caves in a group with a guide.

San Sebastián to Bilbao

San Sebastián, San Telmo Municipal Museum

Plaza Zuloaga 1
Restricted access

Although this museum has nothing on cave art, if you are in the area it is worth a visit not least to experience the beautiful renovated 16th century Dominican convent that houses it. Primarily this is a museum of Basque history, culture and ways of life. There is an archaeological exhibition the highlight of which is probably the exceptional collection of burial stelae dating from prehistoric times to the 19th century.

Ekain (Ekainberri)

Restricted access

Signposted from the small town of Zumaia, approximately 40km west of San Sebastian and inland, the road goes along the spectacular Sastarrain Valley. This cave is one of the best painted caves in Northern Spain and is a must see. It is especially good for children with interactive displays on Palaeolithic life and activities such as painting, hunting and making fire.

The actual cave of Ekain, discovered in 1969, is closed to the public so the visit involves a very realistic life-size facsimile, Ekainberri, together with a very well-equipped state of the art interpretation centre with English displays. Visits are in guided groups (English is available) and involve two circuits, the first in silence to experience the atmosphere and the second with the guide explaining the art. Only one group at a time are allowed in so booking is recommended at busy times.

Excavations within the cave have dated the occupation to 16,500-15,500 BC, the Magdalenian period, and animal bones suggest that it was occupied during the summer. There is also evidence for bears occupying the cave, probably in the winter to hibernate.

The paintings are in red (iron oxides) and black (mainly charcoal) ochres and are spectacular in both their detail and number of animals, mainly horses but also bison and bears. The horses are small with short mains and indications of darker and lighter areas of hide together with other anatomical details, bearing a strong resemblance to wild Przewalski horses of today (see Figure 2.21). The main panel has 11 horses and four bison, and next to it are an adult and a juvenile bear. Some of the animals appear to have 'missiles' stuck into their sides perhaps indicating hunting although bones from the excavation suggest that deer were the most consumed animal.

Figure 2.1. A panel of horses within Ekain (Ekainberri)

The Interpretation Centre is entered past screens that show the paintings and modern animal equivalents. Within the Centre is an extensive presentation of the cave's discovery, its excavation, Ice-Age animals and cave art more generally including other sites to visit. There are also computers with games concerning Ice-Age art (in English).

Cueva de Santimamiñe

Restricted access

Take the BI2338 northwards from the ring road around Gernika-Lumo, turn right on the BI4244 to the car park at the end of the road.

Extensive excavations within this cave have revealed 6m of stratigraphy showing remarkable continuous occupation from the Magdalenian, 14,000 years ago, to the Copper Age, 4,000 years ago. The cave itself is now closed to the public due to deterioration although it is still worth a visit because of the high-tech 3D virtual presentation.

Figure 2.2. A pair of Bison in Cueva de Santimamiñe

The art was discovered in 1916 and comprises nearly 100 depictions either drawn with charcoal or engraved, in three areas of the cave. The highlights are the 32 bison, seven ibex, six horses, one bear and one deer, the main panel is particularly striking with a horse surrounded by seven or eight bison.

Tours are guided (English is available) and it is best to book ahead (if you visit the Archaeological Museum in Bilbao first you can book there). The tour begins at the kiosk adjacent to the hermitage of San Mamés from where you enter the cave mouth for a 15-minute talk on research at the site. On returning to the hermitage you can experience the cave interior and the art through sophisticated 3D virtual reality. The entire 345m length of the cave with its ten chambers has been digitised and you can 'walk' through it using 3D-glasses and see the art.

A curious diversion:

Situated midway between the two caves of Santimamiñe and Ekainberri is the small town of Markina-Xemein, on the BI 633. Just across the bridge at the western-side of the town on the Xemein to Etorbidea road is the little church and hermitage of *San Miguel de Arrechinaga*. This is a curiosity as it is built around three huge megaliths and it has been suggested that these are a dolmen. It is more likely that they are the eroded remains of a natural outcrop but even so the way they fit together and have the altar and a shrine to San Miguel within them makes the place very unusual. Legend has it that a hermit, perhaps St Pollonio, lived here and built his cell between the stones, a reliquary of him is still there, and then a church was built eventually to be replaced by the current one which is 18th century.

Bilbao to Santander

The Archaeological Museum of Bilbao

Calzadas de Mallona, 2
Restricted access

Found in the interesting old quarter of Bilbao, this is a very good museum that presents the archaeology of the Basque region from Palaeolithic to recent times. It is an active research centre with a focus on the conservation and restoration of archaeological materials from all excavations carried out in Bizkaia. It is relatively new, opening in 2008, and across the two-storey exhibition space presents not just artefacts but interesting illustrated panels and interactive displays of analyses and interpretations.

Cueva de Covalanas

Restricted access

Signposted from the N-629 3 to 4km south of Ramales de Victoria, a 650m walk up a steep track from the car park. This was the second cave to be discovered in this area, after Altamira, not a casual find but part of the intensive survey in the area conducted by Hermilio Alcalde del Río in the early 20th century. This was an impressive task, for example around Ramales alone there are over 2,000 caves in the limestone cliffs, six of which contain art although Covalanas is the only one open to the public.

The entrance was excavated but nothing found (supporting the argument for El Mirón being the actual occupation site for the artist(s) here (see below). The paintings start at approximately 80m into the cave and consist of a collection of 18 beautiful red painted deer together with other animals. The consistency of the designs and the use of a distinctive dot technique using fingers and thumb have led to the suggestion that all the art here was done by a single person (perhaps over a short period of time). The highlight here is the freshness of some of the figures looking as if they were done yesterday, also the layout of the art so that it appears that the artist planned what to put where so that visitors to the cave saw figures in a definite order. Near the furthest point is a very provocative place, a small side chamber that will only hold two or three people at a time that contains various paintings including two of the best female deer. It is in this small, confined place that the idea of the animals coming to life is best illustrated – the marrow fat lamps used by Palaeolithic people would burn with a low flickering white light, by simulating this with a partially covered torch the two deer appear to jump and jerk into life.

The cave of El Mirón is situated below Covalanas, take the small path with steps at the sharp corner in the track marked 450m, right on the way down. This large cave (which you can't get in to but can see the interior) has been extensively excavated and shows occupation. It doesn't contain any art but seems likely that this is where the people lived who decorated Covalanas thus making that a 'special' place isolated from the world of the everyday.

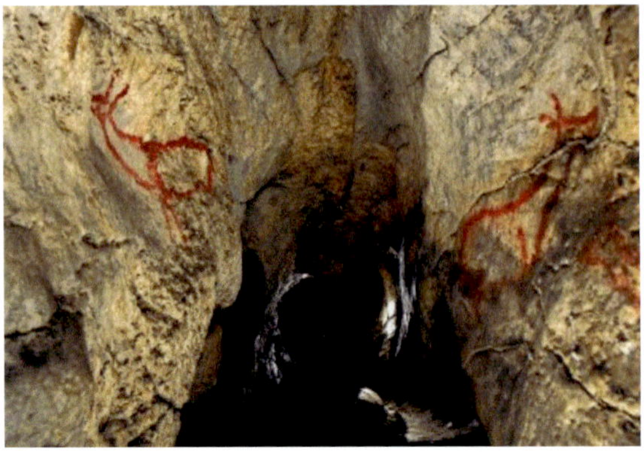

Figure 2.3. A pair of deer in Cueva de Covalanas

Cueva de Cullavera

Restricted access

Signposted from the main road in the centre of Ramales de Victoria, parking near the Coviran supermarket then walk *c.* 400m up the road behind the supermarket, the cave is signposted.

This cave does contain art but it is 1.2km in from the entrance and cannot be visited by the public. Even so it is a spectacular cave with a particularly attractive entrance and gives a good sense of place as you go further into it and consider how far in the prehistoric painters went to carry out their art. The calcitic formations within the cave are spectacular and together with being deep underground add to the sense of other worldliness that Palaeolithic people must have experienced just as we do.

Cueva de Sopeña (Salitre II)

Restricted access

Approximately 30km south-east of Santander the village of Miera is signposted off the CA260 along the CA641. Take this winding road to the church from where the cave is signposted, it's about 3km further where you can park and walk to the cave.

During the Palaeolithic period people occupied the valley of the Miera river in the summer time hunting and fishing. There is evidence for them occupying several caves in the area, the best one for art being Salitre I discovered in 1906. This isn't open to the public but the nearby cave of Sopeña (Salitre II) is a natural cave where the art has been re-created. This comprises two panels, one in red ochre of a hind and possible goat, and further into the cave a black panel with two figures probably a horse and bovid. The art is thought to date to the Solutrean period, *c.* 20,000 years ago.

Within the cave is also the reconstruction of a Palaeolithic campsite and the remains of cave bears which probably hibernated there.

Figure 2.4. A reconstructed campsite in Cueva de Sopeña (Salitre II)

An interesting detour is about 25km south, the:

Cueva de Ojo Guareña

Restricted access

Signposted from the BU-526, and from the centre of Espinosa de los Monteros, this site is in Castilla y León. Continue through the village of Cueva to the car park, then walk and follow signs.

This is a huge complex of limestone caves with over 100km of interconnected underground galleries although only a small part is accessible. There is Palaeolithic archaeology here in the form of paintings and engravings, and of particular interest the footprints of a group of humans preserved in mud who seem to have entered the caves and then left by the same way in about 15,000 BC. Unfortunately, none of this evidence is visible to the visitor although it is still worth going because of the dramatic landscape setting of the caves and to appreciate their internal ambience. At the start of the guided tour is an interesting audio-visual presentation (in Spanish but ask for the English subtitles to be on) which shows the paintings and footprints. There is also mention of a 'Celtic prince' who died in the caves, probably local folklore rather than supported by evidence. However, his skeleton is now in the Burgos Museum, a young man 18 to 20 years old buried with some very nice objects including a fibula and beautifully decorated belt fittings so he does seem to be Iron Age even if not a prince.

As well as the caves here, the visit takes you into the very interesting Hermitage of San Bernabé, a cave with an impressive built medieval frontage including a 13th century carving of St Tirso and some unusual wall paintings. The walk through the galleries takes you past a whole series of medieval silos that have been excavated. Once back at the car park take the path to the Ojo (eye) where the river disappears underground, a place of religious significance in medieval times and perhaps the reason why the Hermitage is here.

Around Santander

Cueva de Altamira II

Restricted access

Located 2km outside the village of Santillana del Mar, signposted to the car park. While here take the opportunity to walk around the medieval village of Santillana with its extremely well preserved buildings and cobbled streets although it does attract a huge number of tourists during the summer. The main street has a series of grand houses dating from the 15th to 18th centuries but the real gem is the 12th century Romanesque Colegiata de Santa Juliana, a former monastery with a beautiful peaceful cloister.

The art in Altamira was the first cave art to be discovered in Europe when in 1879 local antiquarian Don Marcelino Sanz de Sautuola was digging for artefacts after being told about the cave by a hunter a few years previously. It was his eight-year-old daughter, María, who noticed the coloured paintings of bison on the ceiling and her father figured out that they were ancient due to their similarities to art on artefacts that he had seen recently at an exhibition in Paris. It took many years, and the discovery of other art not least in the French Dordogne in 1902, before the international academic community accepted that the art in Altamira was prehistoric. When you see the beauty of the bison and other animals comprising the spectacular 'polychrome ceiling', their composition, the way that they use the natural undulations of the rock to accentuate their shape and postures, it is perhaps not surprising that it was hard to believe that they were painted perhaps 15,000 years ago in the early Magdalenian.

The cave itself is now closed to the general public but in 2001 the museum and interpretation centre were opened together with a splendid facsimile of the cave (la neocueva), a precise replica with explanations in Spanish and English. The original cave has a series of chambers and passages many of which contain art in various forms including not only a range of animals but finger tracings and strange 'masks' which are natural forms 'humanised' by the addition of eyes and other features. The highlight though is the grand polychrome ceiling where ochre, manganese and charcoal have been used to paint red and black animals, mainly bison but also a horse that at 2.5m long is one of the biggest paintings in any of the Spanish caves. Particularly intriguing are the curled-up bison painted onto rock bosses to give them a truly 3-dimensional feel. There are many differing interpretations of these as the posture is unusual, perhaps sleeping, giving birth, dying or dead - the combination of standing and lying beasts together with some engraved human figures does suggest a hunting scene. Studies have shown that there are at least five different phases of art on the ceiling, beginning with simple lined engravings and ending with the polychromes, these final ones being radiocarbon dated to between 14,820 and 13,310 years ago.

The reconstructed cave presents the chamber with the painted ceiling in its original position just inside the cave mouth where excavations in the original one have provided evidence for a long sequence of occupation. This is explained in the replica through the use of audio-visual presentations together with various aspects of archaeology and an explanation of how the paintings were done using original methods. Together with the neocueva is the large museum

Figure 2.5. A polychrome bison in Cueva de Altamira II (© Museo de Altamira. Photo P. Saura)

Figure 2.6. Artefacts from Cueva de Altamira, a flint blade and a bone spear point (© Museo de Altamira. Photo P. Saura)

and interpretation centre which contains a detailed account of the Palaeolithic period, a large range of artefacts many decorated and facsimiles of art from other decorated caves in the area.

It must be said that although the Altamira II experience is very interesting and informative it does lack the emotional connection that is only achieved by visiting a real painted cave. The smell, temperature, silence and darkness of being in a real cave while seeing a painted panel is perhaps as close as we can hope to come to Palaeolithic people even though we will never know why they did this art and what it meant to them.

Monte Castillo (Cuevas del Castillo and Las Monedas)

This large limestone hill overlooking the town of Puente Viesgo contains over forty caves, only two of which are open to view the art, El Castillo and Las Monedas. Two others contain art, Las Chimeneas and La Pasiega, and although not open they are included in the interpretation centre at El Castillo (which must be visited for tickets and tours). Tours and displays are in Spanish. Visits to the nearby cave Hornos de la Peña can also be booked here.

Signposted from the main road, N-623, in Puente Viesgo.

Cueva del Castillo

Restricted access

The interpretation centre has a good display about the cave art of the area plus a small number of facsimiles of decorated portable objects. An interactive display provides images and plans of the four decorated caves.

Extensive excavation in the entrance is still visible and the 20m of stratified deposits cover most of the Palaeolithic period suggesting that the large amount of art within the cave covers a long period of time. El Castillo is remarkable for two reasons, firstly for the large collection of mobile art from the excavations, many engravings on deer shoulder blades (now in the National Archaeological Museum

Figure 2.7. The entrance to Cueva del Castillo (©Emilio Gómez Fernández)

in Madrid, Figure 1.1). Secondly for the long range of time covered by activity within the cave, traditionally the art was thought to cover the Solutrean, lower and upper Magdalanean periods, from *c.* 18,000 BC to *c.* 10,000 BC, the recent end of the range being dated by radiocarbon dates from charcoal used in two bison drawings next to each other (giving 11,110 BC and 10,960 BC). The older end of the date range has been the subject of new research which has raised exciting possibilities – this has traditionally been based on stylistic comparisons with absolute dates being difficult, if not impossible, to attain. In early 2012 dates were published using the new method of uranium-series disequilibrium dating of calcite deposits overlying or underlying the art, thus giving dates after or before the art. Dates were established for art in 11 caves in northern Spain including El Castillo (and Altamira and Tito Bustillo). The results show that the tradition of decorating caves extends back at least to the early Aurignacian period, with minimum ages of *c.* 40,000 years for a red disk, *c.* 37,000 for a hand stencil, and *c.* 35,000 years for an abstract symbol. These minimum ages suggest that cave art was practiced by the very earliest anatomically modern humans in Europe or, and this is where it gets really exciting, that perhaps Neanderthals were also painting caves.

Figure 2.8. A perforated and decorated bone baton from Cueva del Castillo (©José-Manuel Benito Álvarez)

Figure 2.9. One of the many human hand outlines in Cueva del Castillo (©Emilio Gómez Fernández)

The cave is so large and the art so prolific that you only get to see a small fraction, but it is still impressive. There are large decorated panels of animals, one of over 30 human hand stencils, over 100 blown red dots of different sizes along the 'corridor of the dots' plus bison, deer and other animals. A recent

Figure 2.10. A panel of abstract designs in Cueva del Castillo (©Emilio Gómez Fernández)

study of the human hand stencils from El Castillo, 98 in total, has shown that most of them, but by no means all, are male left hands. There are also some interesting examples of using three-dimensionality including a black bison drawn vertically on a stalagmite to capture the 3D effect.

Cueva de Las Monedas

Restricted access

A 600m walk around the cliff from El Castillo brings you to the cave of Las Monedas, so called after 15th century coins were found in it (it was originally called the Cueva de los Osos, Cave of the Bears due to bear bones found on its floors). The cave has some very unusual geological features including some very flat ceilings and large disc-like formations. The art is concentrated in a fairly small area and is all charcoal drawings, it has been suggested that this was all done by one person at one time. The highlight is two beautifully drawn vertical figures of a horse and reindeer back to back.

Cueva de los Hornos de la Peña

Restricted access

Not far from Puente Viesgo and the caves of El Castillo and Las Monedas, on the outskirts of the village of Tarriba on the CA-170, signposted on the left, a steep walk along the track of about 1km to the cave.

The art here is all engraving, except for one painted horse, with some outstandingly natural depictions of horses, bison, aurochs, goats and deer.

Figure 2.11. An engraved horse in Cueva de los Hornos de la Peña

Excavations have shown occupation from Neanderthal times through to the Magdelanian. In the mouth of the cave, an unusual position for art, is a deeply incised horse and as you proceed through the galleries and into various chambers there are other unusual designs – a panel of mysterious macaroni-like symbols, an auroch inscribed into clay in a hollow within the cave wall and a possible snake. In a small chamber at the end of the gallery is the cave's most famous and enigmatic carving of an anthropomorphic figure claimed to be half animal and half woman facing right with one arm raised. A close study of this engraved figure and that of a horse nearby claims that they were both done with the same flint tool (perhaps, therefore, by the same person at the same time?) because of the distinctive tooth pattern on the cutting edge.

Cueva del Pendo

Restricted access

Approximately 10km south-west of Santander in the village of Camargo, signposted from the N611, a winding road then a track to the car park and display board.

This cave is famous for the large collection of mobile art on bone and antler artefacts, including harpoons and pins, discovered during many excavations in its large mouth during the 19th and 20th centuries. Occupation in the cave covers a long period of time from Neanderthals through the later Palaeolithic and the stratigraphic sequence is well displayed. Much of the decorated bone and antler material is now displayed in the museums at Santander and at Altamira.

Figure 2.12. A painted panel in Cueva del Pendo

There are engravings here but the most interesting art is the panel of painted figures in the main chamber, nearly 9m long and only discovered in 1997. This shows eight or nine hinds drawn with dotted and lined outlines and filled with red wash, dated on stylistic grounds to 20,000 to 19,000 years ago. Some of these figures are high on the cave wall and must have needed ladders or something to stand on to be carried out.

San Vicente de la Barquera to Ribadesella

Cueva de Chufín

Restricted access

Signposted from the main A8 Motorway close to San Vicente de la Barquera together with Cueva El Soplau (a spectacular cave but it does not have cave paintings). Take the CA181 following the signs, you meet the guide at the reception area just before the village of Riclones who then takes you to the cave. The tours are in Spanish with a little English.

Beware – this visit involves a walk of about 1k which is along a very narrow rocky path in places and once inside the cave a crawl of 4m along a very low passage. If you can do this though it is well worth it as the cave and art are unusual and impressive. Also of interest is the location of the cave which is appreciated by the approach on foot. The cave looks out over the confluence of two rivers (which are now flooded as part of a dammed reservoir constructed in the 1960s before which the rivers were *c.* 30m lower) which would have served as a route for animals and humans, in the river are salmon and trout together providing a variety of food resources.

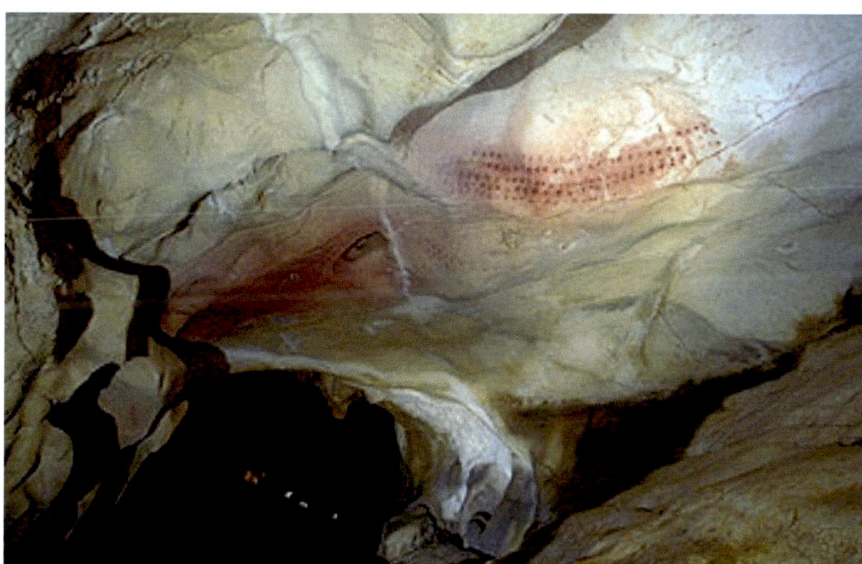

Figure 2.13. A schematic design in Cueva de Chufin

The art in this cave was not discovered until 1972 and it became a World Heritage Site in 2008. In the entrance to the cave is a panel of engravings which are rare in Cantabrian caves (a facsimile is in the Altamira museum). There is a mixture of animals and schematic lines, many overlain, including a very clear complete deer, one of 14. The animals are simple, each comprising two or three lines. Inside the cave, after the 4m crawl, are lines of red dots on either side which may be related (a warning?) to a sudden very deep hole and lake which cuts off the passage. There are other very bright lines of red dots obviously applied by finger tips, in two cases around natural holes/depressions in the rock which the guide suggested represented vulvas. There are also clear red outlines of a bull and horse, some fine engravings including bison and horses, and a very unusual possible female figure with hair, head, body outline and a string skirt instead of legs, an appropriately positioned natural hump in the rock suggests she may be pregnant.

Radiocarbon dating of excavated material in the entrance suggests occupation during the late Solutrian period, *c.* 17,240 years ago. The fine engravings in the interior may be contemporary with this occupation while the engravings from the entrance and the red paintings inside are probably earlier, perhaps late Gravettian or early Solutrean, *c.* 22,000 – 19,000 years ago.

Cueva del Pindal

Restricted access

East of La Franca signposted from the N-634 to the cave and Pimiengo. Continue for about 4km, past the mirador towards sea level, then a 200m walk from the car park. The location is beautiful with views out to sea from the cave entrance but does act as a warning of how different things are now compared to Palaeolithic times when these caves were inhabited and the art produced – for instance, sea level was much lower then, so the coastline was several kilometres further away.

The cave contains a series of art panels, some not open to the public, discovered in 1908 with work in 1957 to clear the entrance and make the cave accessible. The main panel, about 240m from the entrance and nearly 20m long, is a spectacular mixture of mainly red painted animals, with some engravings, including bison, female deer, and a (rare) mammoth. These interact with an intriguing variety of abstract shapes, of particular interest are the claviform (club-like) shapes on the edges of rock shapes and the groups of fingertip dots. Special highlights here are a rare, engraved fish and the mammoth (itself rare other than at Altamira), here with a red dot sometimes claimed to be its heart (so rare that it is used as a symbol for this cave and sometimes Asturian cave art more widely). The art here is dated to *c.* 14,500 to 12,000 years ago.

Between El Pindal and Llanes, just off the main coast road, is an interesting diversion, not cave art but engraved and painted art on a rock face, probably Bronze Age:

Figure 2.14. The rock outcrop of Peña Tú

Ídolo de Peña Tú

Open access

Signposted from the N-634 a few kilometres east of Llanes. There is an interpretation centre (although closed and very derelict looking when we visited in June 2012), signposted from the car park this is a steep but nice walk along a track through the woods for about 1k each way.

Once there it is spectacular with tremendous views southwards over a valley and northwards over the coast. Walk to the end of the crag for the best views. The Ídolo is a rock carving on the face an isolated outcrop of limestone protected by iron railings. It appears to be a possibly cloaked figure with a face, engraved and painted red with a large vertical sword next to it which looks to be Bronze Age. This site is explained in the Archaeological Museum, Oviedo (see below).

Figure 2.15. A copy of the Peña Tú carving and painting

Cueva de La Loja

Restricted access

This cave is situated in the valley of the River Deva about 10km north-west of the small town of Panes off the N621. It has limited opening hours and a visit must be booked at the Tourist Information Office in Panes. There you can ask for directions which will take you along a minor road off the N621before El Mazo.

The cave contains some fine engravings which were discovered in 1908. They stand out clearly in white against the dark rock. There are also some small traces of red paint. The main panel is about 45m into the cave and more than 4m above the present floor level. It features six beautifully engraved animals all facing into the cave, probably five aurochs and a horse. The style of the figures, together with material from excavations within the cave, date them to the Magdalenian period, 14,000 to 11,500 years ago. There is a small interpretation centre.

Cueva de Tito Bustillo

Restricted access

Situated at the western side of the mouth of the Río Sella in Ribadesella, signposted just after the bridge over the river. You need to visit the interpretation centre first where you can get tickets for the cave. The interpretation centre is excellent with interesting displays about how the cave was discovered by local cavers in 1968 and its subsequent excavation. There are also good displays about cave art more widely and Palaeolithic archaeology in general.

Figure 2.16. Paintings in Cueva de Tito Bustillo

Figure 2.17. Painting in Cueva de Tito Bustillo

The cave is about 800m long and you enter through a recent artificial entrance because the original entrance has collapsed. There are several panels of art, engraved and painted, although only one is open to the public (after about 500m) – even so, this is a spectacular display and worth seeing. It is a complex panel of animals representing different phases of art, unusual elements include the large area of red staining which acts as a background for black outlined animals. These are mainly horses with some beautiful outlined and in-filled figures, the use of the colour violet is unusual as are the images of reindeers. Other art which is not accessible to the public is shown in the interpretation centre, including the enigmatic Chamber of the Vulvas.

Excavations in the original entrance of the cave have shown occupation material (explained in the interpretation centre) ending around 12,700 years ago when the entrance collapsed, terminating a long use of the cave and its art which probably started before 20,000 years ago. Excavated material included a good collection of mobile art shown in both the interpretation centre and the Asturian Museum of Archaeology in Oviedo (see below).

Cueva del Buxu

Restricted access

Also, in the basin of the Río Sella, not far from Tito Bustillo although the art here is not as spectacular. Signposted from the A-114 towards Panes, 3km outside Cangas de Onís. Continue to the village of Cardes where there is a wooden signpost indicating the path to the cave, parking here is difficult. It is about a 500m walk up a fairly steep path to the cave.

The cave was discovered in 1916 and was first prepared for tourists in the 1950s with some excavation in the 1970s, all resulting in considerable lowering of the original floor level. Looking at visible stratigraphy as you walk through this cave it is impressive to see how low and constrained access was to the Palaeolithic producers of the art who must have crawled in on their stomachs. The original overhanging entrance has collapsed but still offers great views over the valley below. Artefacts from the excavations indicate occupation in the entrance of the cave, 20,000 to 18,000 years ago, many now in the Asturian Museum of Archaeology in Oviedo (see below).

Art is situated in various panels through the cave starting about 70m from the entrance and containing painted and inscribed forms (the latter sometimes difficult to make out due to the heavily striated natural surfaces). Animals include horses, goats and fallow deer (the latter two both relatively rare in Palaeolithic art), and a whole series of abstract shapes and designs oval, geometric and ladder forms (there are at least 18 roughly rectangular designs similar to those in Tito Bustillo).

While in and around Cangas de Onis it is worth looking at this very unusual site, a dolmen within a church:

The dolmen and church of Santa Cruz

Restricted access

From the main street through Cangas, take the CO-1 side road northwards, past the hotel Santa Cruz on the left and the church and Neolithic dolmen are on the left.

The church is built on the top of the mound of the dolmen. The dolmen was excavated in the 19th century and the chamber can be viewed through a recess in the church floor, it dates to 3,000 – 2,500 BC. The chamber is polygonal and has five large stone slabs and two smaller ones remaining in situ, the tallest over two metres high. Some of the stones have incised art and some badly worn red ochre paintings.

Figure 2.18. The dolmen in the church of Santa Cruz

The original church was built on the top of the dolmen's mound in AD 737 by King Favila I, it was replaced in 1632 and again after the Spanish Civil War when it was destroyed. This site is explained in the Archaeological Museum of Asturias in Oviedo (see below).

In and around Oviedo

The Archaeological Museum of Asturias, Oviedo

Calle San Vicente, 3-5
Oviedo
Restricted access

The museum is located in the refurbished San Vicente Monastery dating back to the 10th and 11th centuries. The building is a World Heritage Site and has been beautifully restored, partly based on excavations. It is located in the old centre of Oviedo, behind the cathedral.

The collections cover all periods of Asturian archaeology and history as well as ethnography. The displays are modern with several good videos although all interpretation is in Spanish. There is an English guidebook available at the reception. The museum includes material from many sites covered in this guide, not least Palaeolithic caves and Castros.

The First Floor covers the Palaeolithic, Neolithic and early Bronze Ages. There is a good display on Neanderthals who arrived in Asturias about 90,000 years ago (the final stages of the Mousterian Culture) based on the very important collection of bones from the excavated cave of El Sidrón which was discovered in 1994. This includes various sorts of tools with a video explaining their manufacture. Because of its importance the Neanderthal collection from El Sidrón has been subjected to extensive scientific research including genetic analysis. This suggests that they may have been redheaded and that their taste buds could detect bitter flavours, they cooked and smoked food. Other evidence suggests that they collected iron oxide to use as red ochre and may have practiced cannibalism on certain occasions.

Modern humans first reached Northern Spain around 38,000 years ago from other parts of Europe bringing with them more developed tools and artistic expression. The section on cave art is impressive with a film showing a range of caves. The display of mobile art showing stone bone and antler pieces with engraved animals and geometric patterns is particularly important for putting the better-known cave art into a wider cultural context.

All aspects of the Palaeolithic world are superbly demonstrated in this museum much of which celebrates the life and work of the Count of La Vega del Sella including many artefacts from his personal collection. During the early 20th century the Count was responsible for establishing archaeology as we know it today in Asturias, not just by writing and collecting but also based on extensive fieldwork. He recognised and named the so-called Asturian Culture which spans the period from the end of the Palaeolithic and the beginning of the Neolithic periods.

The First Floor also includes much good material on the Neolithic, farming and domestication and the beginnings of metal use. There is an excellent video on copper mining and bronze production.

Floor 2 is The Age of the Castros and, again, covers many of the sites mentioned in this book. The origins and developments of Castros are explained, from their beginnings in the 8th century BC through their adoption and adaption into the Roman period. There is a lot of material on the important excavated sites of Chao de Samartín and Coaña (see pages 35 and 41), with a good video. Also, many artefacts, our favourites being the case of small bronze personal ornaments including beautiful brooches, pins and rings and the case of decorated goldwork including torcs which must have been extremely high status.

The internal buildings within Castros are explained in detail including the rather enigmatic 'saunas' for communal, perhaps ritual, use.

Roman Asturias is also covered on Floor 2 as well as a very interesting room on the history of the museum's collection. This includes much information about the Count de La Vega Del Sella, his life and collection including some excellent drawings and paintings of cave art. Medieval Asturias is on Floor 3.

When back on the ground floor be sure to visit the cloisters which are 10/11th century, although parts of the building date back to 761 AD. There is also a room dedicated to World Heritage Sites of all periods in Asturias.

Cueva de La Peña de Candamo

Restricted access

Approximately 35km west of Oviedo on the AS-236 is the town of San Román de Candamo, from the middle of town take the CD-3. The interpretation centre for the cave is along this road on the left and you need to visit here before the cave. From here you can get directions to the cave and also to La Lluera (below).

The interpretation centre provides an excellent introduction to Palaeolithic archaeology and to cave art. It also contains facsimiles of the art in both the caves of La Peña and the rock shelters of La Lluera as well as other sites in Asturias. In the cave itself the main panel is in the principal chamber, it is 8m long and 2m high and contains a complex mixture of paintings and engravings. The colours are red, black and yellow and the animals include deer, bison and horses as well as strange human-like figures. Look out for the famous engraving of a big stag turning its head, pierced by many spears. Around a corner from the main chamber is a very interesting cavity (the camarín) which contains two horses and other figures which seem to have been placed there intentionally to dominate the whole main chamber when lit. Other animals and red discs can be seen around the cavity. The art dates to the Solutrean and Magdalenian periods, 21,000 to 13,000 years ago.

Abrigo de La Lluera

Restricted access

These rock shelters (shallow caves) are on the bank of the River Nalón. If you visit the interpretation centre at La Peña de Candamo you can get directions there, otherwise park at the church in the village of Priorio and it's a 2km walk to the caves. If you can't make this visit there is a good facsimile of the art in the interpretation centre. Priorio is approximately 10km south-west of Oviedo.

This art is unusual to be in rock shelters rather than in deeper caves. There are several along the river valley discovered in the late 1970s, two are open to the public. La Lluera I has the most important art. The art is engraved and appears to be a complex arrangement of animals including deer, aurochs, ibex and bison. Excavation at the mouth of the shelter uncovered a range of material dating to the Solutrean period, *c.* 20,000 years ago.

While in this area it is worth going approximately 30km inland to visit the impressive Prehistoric Park which offers an overview of the Palaeolithic period, cave art and prehistoric archaeology.

Figure 2.19. Engravings in Abrigo de La Luera

Prehistoric Park, Teverga

Restricted access

Take the AS228 southwards from just west of Oviedo, the park is outside the village of San Salvador d'Alesga within the natural park, signposted. You can easily spend a day here enjoying not only the displays and the café, but also the walks through the Asturian mountains.

The displays are within tastefully designed buildings that blend with the natural environment, the main two being the Gallery and the Cave of Caves. The Gallery presents a very good overview of Palaeolithic life through texts, drawings, maps, photographs, multi-media displays, audiovisuals models and reproductions. There are a full range of artefacts both real and facsimiles from many of the caves described above and also from other parts of Europe. Look out for the beautiful enigmatic Venus figurines, carvings of plump women some with curly hair thought to have been fertility symbols. There is also a good explanation of the techniques used to produce the cave art and the walls of the display area are reproductions of cave interiors with art both painted and engraved.

The Cave of Caves is an underground area that recreates the natural setting of painted and engraved art from three caves. The reproductions are full size and the topography of the cave walls have been faithfully reproduced to show the 3D effect of some of the art. The three replicas are of: the polychrome room at Tito Bustillo (see above); the camarín within Candamo Cave (see above) and a panel from Niaux Cave in France.

As well as the exhibitions there are walks around the park, the fenced area with a collection of animals is worth visiting. Here they have collected together a

Figure 2.20. The Prehistoric Park, Teverga

Figure 2.21. Przewalski horses in the Prehistoric Park, Teverga

range of species that are represented in cave paintings. There are various types of deer but also Przewalski and Tarpan horses (both small ancient breeds), European bison and aurochs (ancient ancestors of cattle).

The park also offers a wide range of activities for children, workshops and demonstrations.

Western Asturias
ATLANTIC OCEAN
COSTA VERDE
N
W
E
S
NAVIA
(I)
(M)
GIJÓN
OVIEDO (M)
(I)
GALICIA
CASTILLA Y LEÓN
Rock Art
Castro
(M) Museum
(I) Interpretation Centre

Chapter 3
The Castros of western Asturias

Some of these sites are explained in the Archaeological Museum of Asturias in Oviedo, (page 25), together with artefacts from excavations.

Castros – a brief summary

Castros are stone-built settlements that are a part of the wider hillfort tradition of much of western and central Europe. Castros occur across northwestern Iberia, Spain and Portugal, and this area of western Asturias has some of the best examples to visit. A typical castro has massive stone-built ramparts with one or more entrances enclosing an area which contains stone-built buildings. Some castros, such as Coaña and Chao Samartín were first built in the late Bronze Age, 9th/8th centuries BC, perhaps for primarily sacred/ritual purposes. Within a century or two, in the early Iron Age, they had expanded to become settlements with closely packed roundhouses. People living there had a range of pottery and metal tools, weapons and personal items, there is evidence that they practised mixed farming. One interesting type of structure are the saunas of which each castro seems to have at least one. These have beehive corbelled rooves with a fire at one end and a nearby water tank, usually positioned near the entrance, saunas are thought to be possibly connected with some kind of cleansing rituals.

The Iron Age Asturian tribe, the *Astures*, was conquered by the Roman army led by Augustus Caesar during the Asturian/Cantabrian wars of 29-19BC, by this time the Romans had at least a hundred years of experience of defeating hillforts as they fought their way through France. The Roman army quickly established an infrastructure of roads and agreements with the locals largely based on exploiting the mineral resources of the area, not least the extensive gold deposits. This included taking over the settlements where excavation has shown that the ramparts of castros were generally flattened and existing houses were modified and new ones built. Roman houses tend to be sub-rectangular in shape although earlier roundhouses sometimes have extra rooms added. The Romans continued the tradition of saunas, sometimes modifying existing ones and sometimes building new, larger ones, although whether they retained their ritual significance we don't know. As elsewhere, the Romans had a rich material culture with a much wider range of artefacts, see the interpretation centres at Coaña and Chao Samartín (below).

Around Navia

This route (La Ruta del Castros) takes in eight castros and needs two full days to do it justice. The first three sites described below are west of Navia connected by the N-634, the remaining five are south of Navia along the valley of the Rio Navia connected by the AS-12. If you have limited time the best to visit are Coaña near Navia and/or Chao Samartín just outside Grandas de Salime at the far end of the valley. Both are easily accessible, have undergone considerable excavation resulting in much to see and have a museum/interpretation centre (although both sites have restricted opening hours). The AS-12 has spectacular views over the Navia Valley with extensive forested slopes and reservoirs but be warned that it is a slow road and it can take two hours to drive from Navia to Grandas.

Signposting for these castros is variable as is the amount of walking required, 2km maximum.

Castro El Esteiro

Unrestricted access

This is located 4km to the west of the small fishing town of Tapia de Casariego, it is a coastal promontory fort with tremendous views of the Asturian coastline. It can be reached by walking from Tapia along the coast on the GR E-9 path or by road turning right off the N-634 west of Tapia at Racal Cuarto signposted to Playa de Tapia and Camping, then signposted along a dirt track. There is a display board (in Spanish) at the castro showing a plan of the ramparts and ditches.

The ramparts that cut off the promontory have been seriously damaged by agricultural activity although lengths of them are still impressive either side of the track. Not far from the sign on the right-hand side in the woods are two impressive ramparts and a central rock cut ditch. Minimal excavation in the interior discovered a round house, probably 1st century BC, and subsequent Roman material, although there isn't a great deal to see now. It is worth a visit though because the coastline is spectacular here and it gives a good feel for the isolated location typical of these settlements (if, indeed they were permanently settled in the past, but even if only occasionally settled they are equally impressive). Follow the track to its end and walk to the end of the peninsular and you appreciate how inaccessible this place was to uninvited guests.

Figure 3.1. Castro El Esteiro (photo: Ian Ralston)

Figure 3.2. A notice board at Castro Cabo Blanco (photo: Ian Ralston)

Castro Cabo Blanco

Unrestricted access

Located about 11km east of El Esteiro, the other side of Tapia, this is another coastal promontory fort in a wonderful location with views along the rocky coastline. It also has the biggest, most impressive rock-cut ditch we have seen on a hillfort anywhere! It can be reached on the walking path GR E-9 or by road turning towards the coast from the N-634 in the village of Valdepares. This turn is not signposted but has a Camino de Santiago sign, is where two turns off the N-634 join quickly into one and soon passes the ruins of the Palacio de Fontria on the right, then signposted to Castro y Mirador. The first display board is at the cemetery on the left (in Spanish), the second is further along the track at the outer rampart of the castro. Continue and park by the fence.

There are four ramparts in total, the outer one in the fields is probably Roman, expanding the enclosed area for settlement, there are three Iron Age ramparts with outer ditches cutting off the peninsular. The most impressive of these is just over the fence, to the left the ditch survives to at least 10m deep and 6m to 7m wide, rock cut. As you walk to the end of the ditch look at the rock faces to see tool marks left by the original cutting using small-bladed iron adzes. Excavation has shown that originally this ditch was two metres deeper. Walking to the end of the peninsular crosses another two ramparts and outer ditches and there are various flat areas in the interior which would be suitable for houses. Limited excavation in 2004 dated the first rampart on the peninsular to the 4th century BC. It also revealed an Iron Age roundhouse inside this rampart which was replaced by a Roman house.

Figure 3.3. The massive rock-cut ditch at Castro Cabo Blanco (photo: Ian Ralston)

Figure 3.4. The inner ramparts and ditches at Castro Cabo Blanco (photo: Ian Ralston)

For a good view of the promontory and the fort continue around the track where you have parked to the signposted Campo Redonde where there is a useful explanatory display board.

Castro de Mohías

Unrestricted access

About 10km further east along the N-634, turn towards the coast signposted to Ortiguerra and Playa de Arnelles, turn right into the village of Mohías, follow signs to the castro on the left.

This is an inland promontory fort approximately triangular, with three large ramparts and rock-cut ditches at the point of entry into the interior, near the display board (in Spanish). There are steep natural slopes on the other two sides down to small rivers. The outer, largest, rampart is worth walking along to get a feel for its size. Parts of the interior were excavated between 1968 and 1989

Figure 3.5. Rampart and ditch at Castro de Mohías (photo: Ian Ralston)

Figure 3.6. Roman building foundations inside Castro de Mohías (photo: Ian Ralston)

and the renovated buildings that are still visible (in the interior from the display board), standing to *c.* 0.5m high, are the highlight of this site, more than twenty structures in total. Most of what are visible are probably Roman, *c.* 1st-2nd centuries AD, typically rectangular with rounded corners, some with internal hearths, there are also quern stones lying around. Not far from the structures towards the outer edges of the site some lengths of dry-stone rampart wall are visible suggesting that the whole site may have been enclosed originally. The site started in the Iron Age although little of the interior occupation from this period is visible, one or two round houses can be picked out amongst the Roman buildings.

Castro de Coaña

Restricted access

Take the AS-12 turning off the N-634 in Navia immediately to the west of the bridge over the river, signposted to Grandas de Salime. The Castro is signposted after the village of Coaña.

This is often claimed to be the finest example of a castro in Asturias and it is certainly one of the most impressive in terms of internal buildings due to extensive excavations over the last 200 years or so. Before walking to the site spend some time looking at the informative display in the interpretation centre for explanations of Coaña and the castro culture in general. Make sure you get a plan to take with you to the site. Guided walks are offered at certain times of the year.

Figure 3.7. Aerial view of Castro de Coaña (photo: Ian Ralston)

The path to the site passes a large stone 'bath' on the right-hand side, found in a nearby river this is thought to be associated with water rituals, a similar one was found in the river near the castro at Pendia (below). The path enters through an Iron Age entrance revealed by excavation, what's visible in the trenches isn't easy to interpret but are probably guard chambers. Once within the site following a path made from vertical slabs (probably Roman) the so-called acropolis stands on the high point to the left (access restricted, there has been limited excavation here) and the outer walls run down slope to the right, the densely packed internal buildings are between the two. As with

Figure 3.8. Roundhouses inside Castro de Coaña (photo: Ian Ralston)

Figure 3.9. The outer rampart of Castro de Coaña (photo: Ian Ralston)

other castros, generally speaking the rectangular buildings are Roman and the circular ones are Iron Age (there is an impressive one with walls 3m to 4m high on the right as you enter the interior). As you enter the interior on the left are the two 'saunas' which are pre Roman and subsequently altered to suit Roman tastes, note the corbelled roof and steps in.

It is worth going down slope and walking around some of the outer walls of the castro, note that the whole western area of the site has not been excavated or explored so a complete plan is not available. The highlights of Coaña are firstly the overall impression of the internal layout due to the extensive excavations (over 80 houses are revealed), the detail of some of the stone built houses, the enigmatic rectangular platform on the right as you enter the site, some very large quern or mortar stones left in some of the houses and the possible reasons for the 'acropolis' (social differentiation, a last resort for defence, a special area for religious/ritual activity?).

Castro de Pendía

Unrestricted access

Approximately 12km further along the valley signposted from the road on the left, take the winding narrow road to the bottom of the valley, just over the river the castro is signposted to the right. It's then a 500m walk along the track which was cut in the 1940s but may be the original path to the castro. This site is worth visiting for beside the archaeology there are good views of the very peaceful valley.

Pendía is small, enclosing only 0.5ha and is on a peninsular with three very steep sides, one down to the river, another consisting of a massive stone rampart with outer rock-cut ditch, originally probably 8m to 9m deep, which is on the left as you reach the site. To the north is an enclosure with a single large sub-rectangular building excavated in the 1930s, perhaps for communal use and probably a very early part of the site. The enclosure to the south is

Figure 3.10. The interior of Castro de Pendía (photo: Ian Ralston)

packed with Iron Age round houses and Roman sub-rectangular buildings, this area was excavated between 2006 and 2013. At the northern end is the so-called 'tower', the highest point (not accessible) and appears now as a mass of stones but it does have stone wall faces and structure within it. In the southern part of the site, below the tower, several excavated Iron Age and Roman houses have been partially reconstructed and displayed. Intriguingly one round house near the 'tower' utilises a natural rock outcrop so that inside the house is a shaped bench/shelf.

Of special interest are two 'saunas', buildings with rounded enclosed ends with a corbelled roof at one end showing signs of being heated, together with a stone tank for water. The Iron Age one is close to the entrance from the track and the Roman one, a slightly different shape but the same idea, is further towards the northern enclosure. Also close to the entrance the lower levels of the stone rampart can be seen, dated to the 4th century BC by radiocarbon, with a Roman house built partially over the top of it showing that the Romans probably flattened it.

On leaving the site and returning uphill to the AS-12 note that halfway up at a sharp bend with a bench is a signpost indicating walking to 'Castro de los Mazos'. We failed to find this but even so it is a lovely walk along the track and

Figure 3.11. A sauna within Castro de Pendía (photo: Ian Ralston)

a bonus is that just a few hundred metres along it are good views of Castro de Pendía on the other side of the valley, especially the massive rock-cut ditch. Notice also the impressive deep rock-cut wheel ruts of carts along this track, date unknown.

Castro El Castelón

Unrestricted access

Figure 3.12. The rampart of Castro El Castelón (photo: Ian Ralston)

This is a difficult site to understand and there isn't actually very much to see although what there is are mainly outer walls in places 4m high making them some of the highest surviving in Asturias.

About 20km further along the AS-12, just after the village of Illano, signpost to the left (be careful as this one is easy to miss and it is difficult to park here although there is a grassy lay-by). Follow the track and after about 200m you come to the castro outer wall on the left. This is extremely impressive, a little further on is an original entrance through the wall although it is very overgrown here, it is difficult to proceed further than this. Lower down the slope from here are at least a further two outer rampart walls but these are hard to see and difficult to get to.

Castro San Isidro

Unrestricted access

Approximately 15km further southwards along the AS-12, the castro is signposted to the right. This soon turns into an un-surfaced single track (although not too bad and passable in an average car) which you need to follow for about 8km. It's quite a trek to get there but you are rewarded with staggeringly good views and a castro with some extremely interesting features, some exposed by excavation. Arrival at the castro is indicated by a display board on the right of the track and a grassy car parking place.

Walk from the car park and you encounter one of the important elements of this site, stone 'piedras hincadas' (upright stones sometimes called chevaux-de-frise) which are otherwise unknown in this area, here apparently integrated within the outer counter-scarp bank but in other areas of the site they are free standing upright slabs on rock embedded in the ground and densely packed (interpreted either as defensive in that they hinder attackers, or as enhancing the look of the site as a special place – although, of course it could be both and more). Also in this area is an old excavation trench left open to show the depth of the inner rampart rock-cut ditch and the stone-built rampart front face.

Excavations took place here in 1986 and 87 and the site is dated to the Iron Age with Roman re-occupation probably related to the exploitation of nearby gold

Figure 3.13. Piedras hincadas at Castro San Isidro (photo: Ian Ralston)

Figure 3.14. The rampart face exposed by excavation at Castro San Isidro (photo: Ian Ralston)

sources, Roman mines are known from the area. Several excavation trenches remain open showing the rear faces of the rampart and buildings within the interior. Walking around the ramparts in an anticlockwise direction an inner rampart with outer ditch and then an external counterscarp bank are easily visible. Along this side are two excavation trenches showing good examples of the dry-stone inner face, the stone removed during excavation must have tumbled from the rampart so an approximate height of the original rampart could be worked out. On the far side of the site, past the ruined modern building, is a good area of piedras hincadas. Continuing around the inner rampart you come to a possible blocked entrance showing some original faces and the out turning of the outer bank (all not easy to see due to vegetation). In the interior (not far from the two rampart excavation trenches) are some building foundations.

Castro Chao Samartín

Restricted access

This site is definitely worth the drive as it has a very informative well laid out museum and the site itself has been extensively excavated since the 1990s. Continue into Grandas de Salime (about 14km from San Isidro) and in the centre turn right on the AS-28 to Castro, another 6km, then follow the signposts to the museum. Visits to the site are by guide only and are organised from the museum, there are five tours per day in high season but fewer out of season.

From the museum there is a good view of the castro. There is a 5-minute video (in Spanish, as are all the exhibits in the museum) of the history of the excavations. The upstairs floor contains pre-castro information, Chalcolithic, Neolithic and early Bronze Age. Most of the museum is devoted to a very detailed account of

Figure 3.15. Castro Chao Samartín viewed from the museum (photo: Ian Ralston)

the excavations and interpretation of the castro with many artefacts on display. Chao Samartín is of great importance not least because its long chronology is very well understood, starting with a Late Bronze Age acropolis dated to 800-670 BC, then the castro from the 6th century BC, Roman re-occupation in the 1st and 2nd centuries AD including a large army headquarters house, and a medieval cemetery in the 8th-10th centuries AD.

The site tour is a set route with a guide (some are English speaking) and starts with a length of excavated Iron Age rock-cut ditch and reconstructed dry stone castro wall, originally 4m to 5m high, of the distinctive 'modular' type, i.e. built in sections. There are Roman additions in the form of extra ditches (and probably banks) and a modified entrance with guard chambers. Most of the buildings visible in the interior are Roman (probably modifying and replacing the original Iron Age ones) and include a large sauna-type structure.

Of great interest is the Bronze Age acropolis on the top of the hill where excavations show a double row of postholes, massive timbers forming the internal structure of the rampart encircling the hilltop. Inside the enclosure was a large rectangular building, thought to be for religious/ritual activities including feasting and from which a large 'calendar' was found, now in the Archaeological Museum of Asturias in Oviedo (page 25). Outside the Bronze Age rampart on the top of the hill is a very prominent rock outcrop overlooking a steep natural slope, it has signs of extensive burning at its base, thought to be associated with the activities within the enclosure.

Figure 3.16. The Roman building in Castro Chao Samartín (photo: Ian Ralston)

Roman occupation in the 1st and 2nd centuries AD was both civilian and military, the latter being in a large 'villa' type building and associated with the exploitation of local gold sources. This is the only such building known within a castro in Asturias and had a floor area of 300 square metres, two floors, hypocausts and columns. The whole site was abandoned in the 2nd century AD due to an earthquake which has resulted in a rich collection of artefacts being left behind in the hurry to escape.

Overall, this site is important for four reasons - its long chronological span, the known detail of its construction, its known rapid abandonment and the presence of the Roman villa-type building.

Not a castro but interesting and worth seeing while in the area:

Túmulo del Canadeiro

Unrestricted access

Not far from Chao Samartín is the tumulus (round barrow) of del Canadeiro which is worth a visit if you have 30 minutes or so to spare. Back to the AS-28 and turn right (away from Grandas), the tumulus and Xestoselo are signposted to the left (so are the La Xorenga rock art pictograms).

Figure 3.17. The Túmulo del Canadeiro (photo: Ian Ralston)

The barrow is circular with half removed through agricultural destruction and excavation in 1996 (the first 'excavation' was in the 16th century by permission of the king, this was in fact the first permission for excavation granted in Spain). There is an interesting storyboard showing the development and construction of the barrow and its subsequent history. The barrow itself has a cross section displayed on it to illustrate its structure with two phases and the features excavated within it, the burials date to the Neolithic period, *c.* 4,000 BC and were cremations in pits.

Continue along the road and take the first left, there is a notice board on the left describing the La Xorenga rock art pictograms. These are on the flat rock outcrop on the other side of the road but are not easy to see. There are circular cup marks and schematic human figures pecked into the rock.

If you are in this area you may want to visit two other castros both of which have been excavated and displayed. To the west of Navia is Castro de Os Castros (Taramundi) and to the east is Campa Torres (Gijón).

Figure 3.18. The La Xorenga rock art (photo: Ian Ralston)

Castro de Os Castros, Taramundi

Unrestricted access

West of Navia along the N634 take the N640 to Vegadeo and then the AS-21 to Taramundi. This is a beautiful small mountain village with distinctive stone-built houses. Park in the centre of town, the castro is signposted and only a few minutes' walk away. Note that it may be worth visiting the Tourist Information Office first (restricted opening, five minutes' walk from the castro) as they have a display of replica artefacts from the excavations at the castro, including a very nice dagger with a wooden sheath, as well as other information. They also have audio-guides in English for hire.

The defences of the castro originally enclosed about 2ha of a hilltop but all that is visible now is the excavated area in the interior with several preserved structures. There is a boardwalk and several display boards (all in Spanish) which give good explanations of the preserved archaeology and the excavations which took place in 2004. The enclosure started in the Late Bronze Age, 9th to 7th centuries BC, was extended with a new rampart during the Iron Age and was then extended further in the Roman period. The first board on the walkway explains Structure No. 1, a typical stone-built roundhouse, but notice the circular gullies in the bedrock nearby which represent earlier wooden built

Figure 3.19. Buildings within Castro de Os Castros (photo: Ian Ralston)

houses. Further along the walkway are more roundhouses, generally round for Iron Age and sub-rectangular for Roman, notice that some Iron Age ones have been modified and added to in the Roman period. The final board explains a Roman sauna within which you can see the oven area with a typical corbelled roof. Downslope from here are more excavation trenches but unfinished and covered with plastic sheeting (in 2018), also a reconstructed Roman entrance near the road.

Castro de Campa Torres, Gijón

Unrestricted access
Museum restricted access

This is the biggest hillfort on the coast of Asturias at 30ha enclosed area and is well worth a visit due to its location, museum and reconstructions. It is about an hour's drive east of Navia on the western outskirts of Gijón, 7km from its centre. It is located on Cabo Torres and is signposted from nearby roads. The whole peninsular is an Archaeological and Natural Park with information about birds and flowers as well as the results of several phases of excavation. It sits rather uncomfortably within the industrial landscape of Gijón with massive gas containers nearby and views of the port and coal yards, but don't let that put you off.

There were small scale excavations here as early as 1783 but the main campaign was between 1982 and 1998. From the car park and the reception building the massive, reconstructed stone ramparts are the first things encountered. These were first constructed in the 7th/6th centuries BC but modified several times after that with the latest being 4th century BC. Of interest is the unusual 'modular' construction of these walls suggesting different gangs building them.

Figure 3.20. The ramparts of Castro de Campa Torres (photo: Ian Ralston)

Figure 3.21. Reconstructed Iron Age and Roman houses within Castro de Campa Torres (photo: Ian Ralston)

Going over the central high point the path goes down to the flat area of occupation, the 'plain', where the remains of Iron Age roundhouses and Roman square houses are visible. Note the very unusual stone lined Roman wells. Recent excavation in this area (2022 and 2023) was part of an attempt to alleviate flooding and uncovered new evidence for Iron Age occupation radiocarbon dated to 4th to 2nd centuries BC. Amongst the material recovered were many pieces of daub which formed the walls of the houses, some of which had fingerprints on them.

Approaching the museum, you pass two reconstructions of the two types of house, round and square. The museum, in a converted civil war bunker, has a video (in Spanish) about the hillfort and a good collection of Iron Age and Roman artefacts. The hillfort was known as *Noega* by the classical authors and with the foundation of the Roman town of Gijón in the early 2nd century AD it became depopulated and was abandoned.

Galicia
N
W
E
S
A CORUÑA (M)
SANTIAGO DE COMPOSTELA
PONTEVEDRA
VIGO (M)
OURENSE
ASTURIAS
CASTILLA Y LEÓN
PORTUGAL
Petroglyph
Menhir
Dolmen
Castro
(M) Museum
(I) Interpretation Centre

Chapter 4

Coastal Galicia

Galicia is the spectacular north-western corner of Spain. Inland the terrain is mountainous and offers great opportunities for walking despite large areas of indigenous forest being replaced by eucalyptus plantations which in places are spreading out of control. The Galician towns and villages are distinctive often with granite buildings and slate rooves, the most well-known being the beautiful medieval Santiago de Compostela which is a must to visit. An important aspect of the Galician identity is its language, Galego, which after being suppressed by Franco is now making a big come back and is widely spoken. Various signs will often have both Castillian and Galego and here we use whichever we have seen when finding sites which can be confusing.

We concentrate on the coast (approximately!), travelling from A Coruña in the north, westwards then southwards finishing around Vigo and the Portuguese border. Galicia's coastline is wild, battered by the Atlantic and its storms and often having wet and cloudy conditions even in summer, so be prepared. The coast consists of many large and small rías which are inlets and estuaries with cliffs and relatively protected sandy beaches often extensive and not at all crowded. Fishing is important in Galicia and the coast is peppered with fishing villages and some larger towns offering a wide range of excellent seafood.

The prehistoric archaeology of Galicia is as varied and as fulfilling as its food. The three main monument types you are likely to encounter, as reflected below, are rock art (petroglyphs), megalithic tombs (dolmen) and hillforts (castros). Each one of these types has at least one main site with a museum explaining the monument type in a wider context. For rock art it is the Archaeological Park at Campo Lameiro, for megalithic tombs it is Dombarte and for castros it is Santa Trega, all are described below. These three are obviously the best to visit if you want more extensive and detailed information while many other sites lack any interpretative information at all but are in beautiful places and often involve nice walks. If you want a good beach, a café/bar and an excellent castro that has been excavated and partially reconstructed then we recommend Baroña.

We start in the city of A Coruña itself with a tremendous castro and a good museum:

The Archaeological and Historical Museum, Castillo de San Antón

Paseo Marítimo Alcalde Francisco Vázquez, 2
Restricted access

It is worth visiting this museum before going to the castro as it has a comprehensive collection of material from the excavations there. You can also book your visit to the castro from here. Signposted from roads around the port.

The museum is within the castle situated on what used to be an island. The castle itself is impressive as are the museum's collections which cover more than archaeology. Archaeology is on the ground floor and covers the full span of Galician material from the Neolithic to the Romans and beyond. There is a range of material from the excavations at the castro including pottery, weapons and tools. Look out for the spectacular gold objects known as the Treasure of Elviña.

On exiting the ground floor you can see the rock-cut cistern used to supply the castle with water. Also there is the 'Borna', a replica of an Iron Age boat. In the upper patio garden is a reconstruction of a dolmen and also some petroglyphs on a slab of rock moved from their original location.

Castro de Elviña

Elviña University Campus
Restricted access

This is located on the southern outskirts of the city, in the university area. From Avenida de Alfonso Molina you can access the Elviña campus in the direction of the University Campus of Zapateira, follow the signs. Visits are in guided groups and can be booked at the archaeological museum above.

This impressive castro is one of the largest in Galicia with an enclosed area of over 4ha and there is much to see here due to excavations which have been ongoing for many years. It is located on a prominent hilltop with good views over the modern city and the coastline. The castro was constructed in the 3rd century BC and remained occupied until the 4th century AD when it was an important Roman settlement.

The castro consists of three connected walled enclosures, the highest, the croa, retains its dry-stone walls with an entrance to a height of around 5m which are very impressive. The lower enclosure walls are not so high. Inside there are various buildings which are houses and other buildings of various kinds both Iron Age and Roman. Most domestic structures are within the croa and here it is possible to see the development of house forms from simple circular Iron Age houses with no internal divisions, through oval shaped larger structures to square and rectangular Roman buildings with different rooms and spaces. Some houses have preserved internal features such as hearths.

Figure 4.1. Castro de Elviña

As well as houses there are other buildings of interest especially on the first terrace. Close to the wall is a large oval building divided into three rooms one of which has a series of altar stones suggesting that it was a structure where religious/ritual activities took place. At the gate into the croa is an interesting spring which seems to have been developed into a watering hole. Look out for the rock-cut well/cistern with steps down to it located on the second terrace, it is 12m long and 6m deep and a very unusual feature within a castro.

Dolmen Pedra da Arca

Unrestricted access

West of A Coruña, off the AC414 and 2.5km outside the town of Malpica. Take the track signposted to Camping Sisargas, park at the campsite and take a nice walk down the track through the pine forest. The tomb is on the right within trees after about 400 metres, visible if on foot but you may miss it if you drive.

Figure 4.2. Dolmen Pedra da Arca

The main chamber is well preserved with six uprights, the entrance faces east. The massive capstone is broken and some of it is missing. Parts of the cairn survive as a mound of smaller stones around it.

Croa do Castro

Unrestricted access

Not far out of Malpica on the AC414 road to Carballo, this site is signposted from the road. Follow the minor road and it is signed left after the second sign. The site is visible as a flat-topped isolated hill within agricultural land. Around the top of the hill is a much-denuded earthen rampart steep on the outer side into a large ditch. In places are traces of stone wall faces on the outer side of the rampart. The interior has been ploughed flat so there isn't much to see. On one side is a possible entrance gap.

Dolmen de Cabaleiros

Unrestricted access

This site deviates inland from our coastal focus a little and is a little tricky to find, even so if you are going that way anyway it is worth seeing. From Carballo take the AC414 south to Anxeriz then left on the AC400 towards Silva, then a right signed turn at A Pedro del Salgueira, keep going and the site is on the outskirts of Pontepedra. It is in a walled enclosure on the side of the road and is well preserved with a sizeable mound/cairn with kerbstones, seven uprights and a capstone.

Figure 4.3. Dolmen de Cabaleiros

Castro 'A Cidá' de Borneiro

Unrestricted access

Note: this site is very close to the Dolmen de Dombate and the two can easily be visited together.

Signposted on the AC430 between Ponteceso and Baio, there is a car park on the road. Follow the signs along the track. A board shows a 10km walking route around the area which takes in another castro, Castelo de Borneiro, we just did A Cidá for which you take the path to the right over the stream. There is another board here with details of the excavations, in Spanish.

Walk up the path to the site which is on the top of a low hill mainly covered in Eucalyptus but with some indigenous oak and some very impressive lichen. The settlement is approximately oval, encircled by a massive stone wall originally 5m high and 4m wide, external ditch and packed full of stone-built houses in the interior with walls surviving up to 2m high in places. The structures are mainly circular although there are some rectangular ones, some have central hearths and other internal features. The site was discovered in 1924 and has been extensively excavated in the 1930s, 1960s and 1980s and the buildings and parts of the external wall and entrance are largely consolidated and reconstructed.

The entrance is particularly interesting and impressive. It is a typically narrow stone-built passageway but has some associated buildings. One is a large oval shape with a cut bedrock surface, a stone drain, niches in the walls, a sluice-gate type of structure, steps down into it and a possible corbelled roof. This appears to be something to do with water control and may be a 'sauna', a type of building well known within Asturian and Galician castros. It may be significant that it is within the entrance complex, perhaps for 'cleansing' as you enter the settlement?

Figure 4.4. Houses within Castro 'A Cidá' de Borneiro

Figure 4.5. The entrance passageway of Castro 'A Cidá' de Borneiro

The excavations have yielded a range of material culture including millstones, whetstones, metal moulds for casting, a range of pottery, needles, rings, fibulae, knives, daggers and sickles together with evidence for the consumption of fish and shellfish. Radiocarbon dates show occupation starting in the 6th century BC making this one of the earliest castros in Galicia.

Dolmen de Dombate

Dolmen and museum
Restricted access

Signposted from the AC-430 and CP-1404. There is a car park.

Visit the museum first, the displays are in Galego and Castillian but there is an English leaflet which you need to ask for at the reception desk. The display includes a good general background to the Neolithic period and megaliths in particular, generally the 5th to 3rd millennia BC up to the beginnings of the Bronze Age. There are small collections of various artefacts but the main focus is the life-size reconstruction of the Dombate chamber and the very unusual art found on some of the upright stones. This comprises both engravings and red, white and black paintings, depicting a range of geometrical patterns in lines and zones together with dots and wavy lines. There is also a set of large enigmatic engravings that look curiously like jugs and water. The paintings were only preserved on the lower parts of the stones and it isn't known whether they were originally more extensive, either way they are a rare example of painted megalithic art.

The actual monument is in the other building which is rather ugly and overpowering but designed to protect the monument. As you walk around inside it there are further display boards and cutaway sections through the

Figure 4.6. Art on the reconstruction of Dolmen de Dombate

reconstructed monument which give a good idea of its internal structure and how it was built. Excavations in the late 1980s show that there are actually two megalithic tombs here, the earlier one is smaller with a kerb approximately 10.5m in diameter and a chamber oriented east-south-east measuring 2.4m by 1.9m. Originally there were nine uprights although few remain and very little was found in the chamber, this phase is undated.

The second phase tomb is bigger with a mound of 24m diameter that seems to have been originally only 1.8m high so that it didn't cover the stones of the chamber which must have protruded from the top. This is an interesting point as it may explain why virtually all other dolmen across Spain have low mounds/cairns. The chamber is polygonal and of seven uprights with a massive capstone and is approached from the east by a 4m long corridor of uprights which decrease in height towards the entrance. Other than the paintings and carvings, another intriguing feature of this tomb is a line of 20 carved 'idols', some anthropomorphic, placed across the entrance.

Based mainly on the wide range of artefacts found within the tomb it is dated from 3,900 BC to 2,700 BC. These include early flint blades, polished stone axes and a range of pottery. The final act, in 2,700 BC, seems to have been the blocking of the entrance with a massive stone.

Figure 4.7. The Dolmen de Dombate

Castro das Barreiras

Unrestricted access

On the outskirts of Vimianzo on the C-552 to A Coruña/Finisterre, the site is situated on the left-hand side of the road when leaving Vimianzo and is difficult to miss. This is a massive oval earthwork comprising a bank up to 8m high and an outer ditch, measuring 110m by 65m internally. A section is missing near the road having been flattened and this is probably where the original entrance was. It is worth walking around the top of the earthwork to get a sense of the landscape setting of this site which is unusual in being low lying, a location which may be responsible for its larger than average rampart. In places stonework can be seen within the bank suggesting that it was originally a massive stone-built rampart.

Near the road is an information board, in Spanish, which describes a small excavation in 2010 in the interior of the enclosure. Within a very small area evidence was unearthed for three stone buildings together with over 500 sherds of pottery and iron artefacts dating to the 2nd century BC.

The Route of the Dolmen (La Ruta dos Dolmen)

Six dolmen, all unrestricted access

Along the AC-552 about 1km outside Baio on the way to Vimianzo the Ruta dos Dolmen is signposted along a minor road to the left. On the corner is a board showing a map of the route with the six dolmen, it is 43km in total. You need to follow the signs around the route, in general this is fairly straightforward although there are some quite long lengths without signs and it is easy to think that you are lost – keep going! The route is mainly along small country lanes through small fields and Eucalyptus plantations and is very peaceful and worth doing even if you don't visit all six dolmen.

1. Dolmen Pedra Cuberta

Signposted with a plan of the site. Take the right-hand path close to the road, the site is difficult to see as it is partly overgrown which also makes it difficult to interpret. There is some cairn material still in place, several uprights of which two large ones could be an entrance, a single capstone although others are probably missing. The site was reportedly excavated by German archaeologists in 1933 although we have no further details of this.

Carry on along the signposted route through more plantations and past the church at San Miguel de Treos. The next dolmen, Pedra Moura, is a signed right turn off the main route. When you have visited this one return to the main route.

Figure 4.8. Dolmen Pedra Cuberta

2. Dolmen Pedra Moura (de Carneo)

Off the main route, signposted with a site plan, overgrown in a field 200m on the left down the track. The chamber is about 4m long, has 11 uprights and is partly collapsed, there are two large capstones.

Re-trace your steps to the main route and turn right.

3. Dolmen Pedra de Lebre (aka Anta de Serramo)

In the woods at the sign on the right-hand side of the road. This site does not have a site plan as the others do and is quite difficult to spot in the undergrowth. Orientated to the east, it has three dislodged capstones and several uprights, two of which are curiously at right angles to the chamber. Only discovered in 1987 by a local archaeologist.

Continue along the road, the scenery is beautiful and the vegetation lush with blackberries, bracken, holly and dark and light pink heather.

4. Dolmen Arca da Piosa

This monument is a c. 5km drive along an unmade road through the forest, signposted at the start, it's a bit rough in places but well worth the effort as it is one of the best. It has a large circular cairn which together with the chamber and entrance passage are well preserved. There are two large capstones still

Figure 4.9. Dolmen Arca da Piosa

in situ, one covering the chamber which is about 3.2m long and the other the passage of about 1m. There are also six large uprights and it does suggest, as at Dombate (above), that originally these projected out of the cairn to be visible. According to local legend this is the burial place of the warrior Brandomil.

Retrace your steps back through the forest to the main road, turn left following the route to Baiñas. In the village go across the junction following the signs.

5. Dolmen Pedra da Arca (aka Casa dos Mouros)

The final sign has a site plan from where you follow the path. This dolmen is in good condition with a considerable nearly circular cairn approximately 30m in diameter with possible kerbstones visible in the undergrowth in places. It has three large overlapping capstones covering two chambers in total about 7.5m long. The remains of uprights define a corridor orientated to the east. It is claimed that archaeologists investigating this site found paintings inside the burial chamber (similar to Dombate, above) although we could see no sign of them.

Continue along the signed route. For the final site you need to park and walk along the track through the woods, it's about 1km and a nice walk which is rewarded with a very unusual dolmen.

6. Dolmen Casota de Fréans (aka Casota dos Mouros)

The design of this is completely different to the others on the route, and indeed it is unusual within Galicia. It is made from thin slabs, four in total comprising the capstone, two sides and rear to produce a rectangular chamber nearly 3m

Figure 4.10. Dolmen Casota de Fréans

long. Due to the relative simplicity of its design compared to many other sites it has been suggested that it is early in date and in the developmental sequence of dolmen. There are possible cup-marks, circular hollows that are thought to represent some form of Neolithic symbolic art, on the outside of the left-hand side slab and on the inside of the right hand one (as you look into the entrance). The 'room-like' character of this site must have attracted attention over the years and it is easy to imagine it being used for all sorts of things, not least a shepherd's hut. Indeed, at the rear of the side slabs are grooves which may be to hold up a shelf.

Note the fantastic long-distance views from the entrance over the valley to the hills beyond. The location and setting of dolmen has been much discussed and it is clear that they were often sited to be both visible from a distance and to offer good views outwards, perhaps for the dead who were buried there and for the mourners taking part in ceremonies around the monument.

A diversion to Santiago del Compostela

If you are in Santiago, and you probably will be, and want a change from impressive medieval buildings, then on the outskirts are a castro and a panel of rock art.

Castro de Conxo and petroglyphs

Unrestricted access

This site is not easy to find but rewards perseverance. Take the old road to Pontevedra, the N550, out through the suburbs of Santiago. By the hospital, just before a large traffic island, on the right-hand side is signposted 'petroglifos', pointing along a small track between the island and Lidl supermarket. Park on the track and continue on foot for about 50m then take a small footpath to the right which goes up hill and has a wire fence on the right-hand side. The rock art is on a large nearly horizontal slab of bedrock before the top and near the fence. There are a variety of symbols carved into the rock including daggers (of early Bronze Age type), a large 'face' or 'cart' design (you decide which!) and 'ladder'-like patterns.

The castro is on the top of the hill but there is nothing much to see other than to appreciate its location and high setting with good all-round views.

West of Santiago on the coast is the small town of Muros and the nearby village of Louro, both of which have access to petroglyphs. If you only have time for one of these the group from Muros are the best.

Figure 4.11. Castro de Conxo petroglyphs

Petroglifos Cova da Bruxa

Unrestricted access

Take the AC400 northwards from the centre of Muros. About 1km after the cemetery on the left turn left along a minor road, after about 700m park and walk along a path to the right towards the Mirador de los MiniOnTour-Cova da Bruxa, the petroglyphs are as far again on the right. The views are spectacular and this is a nice track to walk along.

There is an information board in Spanish. The site is large with several slabs of granite bedrock having carvings so you need to look around. The best is covered with spirals, human and animal figures, abstract designs and a very strange symbol that looks like a supermarket trolly!

It is possible to walk to the following site following paths across the mountain but this is about 5km. To drive return to Muros and follow the coast road round to Louro.

Figure 4.12. Laxe das Rodas petroglyphs (Photo: Simon and Barbara Maddison)

Petroglifos Laxe das Rodas

Unrestricted access

Go north out of Louro on the CP5032 for about 1km. You can park on a track to the right where a path goes to the left to the site which is a large outcrop of granite about 100m on the left. There is no information board.

There are a series of mainly spirals and loops carved into the rock some with pools incorporated within them (best seen after rain when they are full of water). There is a network of other pools and grooves but whether these are natural or not is hard to tell. However, when seen in the wet it does seem to emphasise the importance of flow and water (or perhaps another liquid).

Take the AC550 coast road south from Neia to reach one of the most spectacular castros but stop on the way to see an impressive panel of rock art.

Petroglifos de A Gurita

Unrestricted access

Heading south, just before the castro turn left following a small sign for petroglifos, there's a couple of signed turns along small roads and about 400m after the last one is a broken display board on the right. Park here and follow the footpath up slope for about 50m. To the left look for a sloping large slab of bedrock, not easy to spot but it looked black to us, part way up the hillside. There is a fairly steep path up to the slab which is completely covered with carved symbols, a very impressive example of Galician rock art. You need to move all around the slab to appreciate it although this isn't easy to do. Plainly visible are deer, spirals, circles with dots and a range of geometric patterns. The views are also good here stretching out along the coastline and out to sea.

Return to the coast road, the AC550, turn left and in a short distance you reach the Castro de Baroña on your right which is well signposted.

Figure 4.13. De A Gurita petroglyphs

Castro de Baroña

Unrestricted access

There is parking, a café/bar and access to a good beach and beautiful stretch of coastline. At the information point you can get a leaflet in English, there are also information boards nearer the site with some English on them.

Follow the footpath to the castro which is built on a striking rocky peninsula linked to the mainland by a small sandy isthmus. Note the wheel ruts in the bedrock as you walk towards the castro, about 1m apart, date unknown. There are good views of it as you approach which enable an appreciation of its siting and layout. You first reach the massive outer rampart which cuts off the isthmus, this is a stone wall with a very impressive rock-cut ditch. As with the inner rampart and the internal structures, this outer rampart has been heavily reconstructed although it is based on excavated evidence and very well done giving a good impression of what it might have been like originally.

Carry on to the inner rampart, another massive stone wall, double in places and at least 5m wide and with internal steps so that you can walk along the top. Access is through a single corridor-type entrance with a slabbed floor which would have originally been closed off with massive wooden gates. Just inside the entrance to the right notice an old excavation trench in which you can see the original wall and its foundations. The interior is divided into a lower and upper part both suggesting dense settlement with numerous circular, oval and sub-rectangular buildings packed in together and now represented by

Figure 4.14. Castro de Baroña

reconstructed lower walls up to about 1m in height and some features such as doorsteps and hearths. In places the original bedrock pathways between the structures are visible. Originally these buildings would have had wooden and thatch rooves and been a mixture of dwellings, store-rooms, workshops and other buildings. There is excavated evidence for the numerous activities that you would expect for a vibrant settlement such as this including metalworking, pottery and weaving. These people were farmers with evidence showing a range of crops and animals and also the importance of fish and shellfish which you would expect for such a coastal location. From the upper area you can climb to the cliff tops to get a good view of the site and coastline.

From Baroña carry on south along the AC550 to reach the next site.

Figure 4.15. The interior of Castro de Baroña

Figure 4.16.
Dolmen de Axeitos

Dolmen de Axeitos (aka Pedra do Mouro)

Unrestricted access

A very well-preserved tomb that rewards a visit. At San Martiño de Oleiros follow the signs from the AC550, the tomb is situated in a nice small walled wooded park. Some remains of the original covering mound/cairn within which is a well-preserved chamber, polygonal in form with eight uprights leaning inwards and a big capstone which is about 3.5m x 4.5m. Three smaller uprights suggest a possible entrance passage oriented towards the east which is usual for these monuments. It has been noted that this site has been dug into but we could find no information about the results.

The next group of sites require going inland and climbing into the spectacular Sierra de Barbanza. Once at the top the terrain is fairly flat and easy going with heather, gorse and grasses much of it grazed by horses. The sites are spread over a wide area and can be reached by small roads and tracks although it is an ideal place for walking with tremendous, long distance views. Make a day of it!

The Barbanza megalithic landscape

Unrestricted access

Before visiting this area it is worth going to the small museum at Neixón where there is information about walking routes and monuments (see below).

From Boiro take the old road signposted to Noia, the DP1105. About 2km after the village of Cures at a small hamlet called Moimenta turn left signposted to Dolmen on the EVA No. 10, then to the right at the sign 'Ruta das Mamoas. Conxunto megalítico'. This is a long winding road to the top, go past the military installation and continue along the minor road until the information board on the right of the road where you can park. The board describes the walking trail (in Spanish) and some of the archaeology which covers about 5km and will take about two to three hours although it is possible to drive to certain points then get out and walk around several monuments. We took the drive/walk option as described here. If you choose to walk the whole route we think it is marked by wooden posts with yellow and white tops although these aren't always obvious.

Start by crossing the road from the board, going down the road signposted to Lidon then taking the track off to the right. Large circular cairns are obvious, there are two to the right of this track, but this is a megalithic landscape and some of the features are much less obvious. As you walk along this track look out for lines of stones, some up to about 1m high, which are the possible remains of Neolithic field boundaries. There is a good one to the left of the track which runs for many hundreds of metres. You will reach the road and can either return and drive or walk on.

If driving branch right where signposted and stop at Board 2 where there is a dolmen with much of its cairn left, a good chamber of uprights and a broken capstone. There are some interesting modern 'petroglyphs' inside the chamber! Opposite Board 2 is a track which leads to large cairn with many of its included upright stones and capstone gone. Nearby another post marks the position of a 'trough' cut into the rock, thought to be Neolithic in date but of unknown purpose.

Figure 4.17. One of the Dolmen at Barbanza (Photo: Simon and Barbara Maddison)

If driving, carry on along the road from Board 2 then take an unmade track to the right (not signed) where, at a curve, is a cairn with dolmen on the right. The cairn is in good condition with a nice small chamber although the capstone has gone. There is another to the left of the track, again a good cairn with some uprights although the capstone has gone. Just down the slope is a very interesting linear bank with stone facing which illustrates one of the problems in trying to interpret large areas of landscape such as this mountain top. This stone bank could well be Neolithic, equally it could be a medieval or post-medieval land boundary and if of these later dates it could be re-using an earlier original. In these upland areas construction techniques for field walls and other types of boundaries probably haven't changed much since prehistoric times being based on local resources, that is stones.

Within the Barbanza area there are other dolmen and other prehistoric features, we didn't visit them all. In a way this isn't critical for what is important here is to get a feel for the landscape, which probably wasn't very different in prehistoric times, and to imagine it as a lived-in place. People were farming this area, perhaps mainly sheep and goats due to its altitude, living here although settlements are not known and certainly burying their dead within dolmen that were an integrated part of their daily landscapes. This is what landscape archaeology is all about rather than looking at a single monument devoid of its surrounding context.

Back to the coast for the next site, an archaeological interpretation centre and castros situated on a promontory within the bay of Rianxo with some rock art on the way there. From Boiro take the coastal road the DP1101 and then the DP1106.

Petroglifo Pedra das Cabras

Unrestricted access

Just before the small village of Quintero a small road to the left is signposted Petroglifo (very easy to miss so look out for it) and it is worth taking this slight detour. Follow the road, signposted to the right, after about 100m there is a parking place and an interpretation board on the right (by a very nice medieval stone cross). Walk up the path and you will see a large sloping slab of bedrock. The engravings are clear in the centre of the slab, two deer facing right with legs and antlers.

Go back to the main road, the DP1106, turn left and soon you will see the signs for the Archaeological Centre and Castros de Neixón. Follow the signs through the back streets to the sea, at the roundabout turn right and park by the centre.

Figure 4.18. Pedra das Cabras petroglyph

Archaeological Centre and Castros de Neixón

Centre restricted access
Castros unrestricted access

Visit the small interpretation centre first. It has information on many prehistoric sites in the area including the Barbanza landscape (above), as well as details of the castros here.

This peninsula is a lovely place with indigenous oak woodland (no eucalyptus!) and views across the bay and along the coast. There are two castros here both cutting off the peninsula with a single massive rampart, an earlier and smaller one towards the end of the peninsula and a larger later one which you encounter first. There are information boards (in Spanish) at various places along the walk with some good reconstruction drawings. Take the path through the picnic areas and you come to the outer rampart which is massive and shown by excavation to have a 6m ditch cut through bedrock on the outside of it. Inside the rampart is an area of excavation which has revealed stone-built roundhouses, a possible metal working area and other structures, all of which were being conserved when we visited. This larger castro was first constructed in the 5th century BC and remodelled and refurbished in the 2nd and 1st centuries BC and eventually abandoned in the 3rd century AD perhaps due to Roman hostility towards the inhabitants.

Keep walking towards the end of the peninsula and you see another massive rampart cutting of the end portion of the land. Inside the rampart is an excavated

Figure 4.19. Information board showing the two Castros de Neixón

area showing the stone inner face of the rampart and three partial stone-built roundhouses. This smaller castro was built and inhabited during the late Bronze Age/Iron Age transition period, 6th century BC, and was then replaced by the larger settlement.

Standing on the rocks at the very end of the peninsula you really appreciate what a fine place this would have been to live, not just for the views but for access to both land and marine resources.

Castro de Cidá

Unrestricted access

Further west along the peninsula on a hill to the west of Ribeira is this magnificently sighted castro. Off the minor road CP7301 take the road to the Miradoiro (viewpoint) Pedra da Rá, enjoy the views over the coastline and from here follow the path on the other side of the road to the castro.

This site is another fine example of how Iron Age people carefully chose strategic locations to build castros maximising their views.

There is a rather tatty notice board. The ramparts are difficult to see being largely overgrown but impressive if you can find them. There is a large area

Figure 4.20. Castro de Cidá (Photo: Simon and Barbara Maddison)

of excavated and conserved houses showing various forms and sizes including roundhouses and oval ones which are probably Roman. To the left when within the excavated area is an unusual rectangular building overlying two oval ones.

Back inland continuing south towards Pontevedra is the Centre for Rock Art at Campo Lameiro which is a must see. On the way you can visit a very unusual menhir, a single standing stone. Take the main road to Pontevedra, the N550. Turn off in the direction of Cuntis and A Estrada and just before Cuntis turn right signposted to Moraña and Campo Lameiro, the PO226. From the centre of Moraña the Archaeological Park is signposted, the PO221. On this road is signposted the Gargantáns Menhir, turn right and right again.

Menhir Lapa de Gargantáns

Unrestricted access

The standing stone is now conical with a square base and about 2m high although it may have originally been higher and has been broken and probably moved. There is an information board (in English) which is very informative and describes zig-zag carvings and cup mark decorations on the stone. These are mainly difficult to see although some of the cup marks are clear. The purpose of single standing stones such as this one is not known despite them being relatively common across many parts of western and northern Europe. A popular theory is that they were some kind of marker stones perhaps indicating routes.

Figure 4.21. Menhir Lapa de Gargantáns

Return to the PO221 and follow the signs to the Archaeological Park at Campo Lameiro. The village itself is very attractive and the Park is on the outskirts, a rather convoluted route being well signposted.

Archaeological Park of Rock Art (Campo Lameiro)

Restricted access

Note: it is always best to view rock art in the early morning or the evening when the sun is low and the engravings are enhanced by low shadow.

There is a car park and café. The Interpretation Centre is excellent and offers a detailed explanation of rock art and wider aspects of prehistoric archaeology. There is an introductory video in English (you can ask at the reception desk for it to be shown). The

Figure 4.22. Rock art at Campo Lameiro (©Archaeological Park of Rock Art, Campo Lameiro)

displays are not in English. Various sections cover all aspects of rock art, techniques, types, distribution across Europe, as well as archaeological techniques such as radiocarbon dating and using 3D scanners. All are extremely modern and well-done including reconstructions of houses, artefacts, domestic life, metal production and the use of dolmen in disposal of the dead. Particularly intriguing is the second video room which has three screens and explores the possible meaning of rock art (always a very hotly debated topic!). Here, suggested uses are to do with hunting, shaman entering trances and increasing the prowess of warriors, all involving complex methods of visual communication before the use of writing.

Outside is a marked trail that takes you around a whole series of rock art panels which are in situ. There is a good leaflet in English which shows the route and gives interesting information about the history of discovery of the art. The rock art locations are numbered and there are three on the main route and a further six on longer routes. It is an easy walk along good paths through thin woodland. Seeing so many locations together gives a good feel for the landscape setting of this art, whether they are positioned to be seen from a distance or nearby only. It is obvious that there are many possible locations with suitable rock surfaces that were not chosen to be decorated implying something significant for those that were.

A wide range of motifs are represented here in the art. Our particular favourites were No. 2 and No. 3 where there are at least six large spirals and a whole host of animals. No. 5 is worth visiting because it has a mirador (a viewing platform) which offers spectacular long-distance views. No. 9 is interesting and different as it is a reconstructed prehistoric village with two roundhouses, a rectangular house and outbuildings made from wattle and daub and thatch, it's very well done and used as a teaching resource for children.

Figure 4.23. A reconstructed roundhouse at Campo Lameiro

Further south and on the coast is Galicia's largest town of Vigo which developed around a spectacular castro:

O Castro Vigo

Castro unrestricted access
Museum restricted access

This is situated in the centre of Vigo on the slopes of O Castro Mountain and is a very attractive park covering about a square mile with nice walks, trees and flower beds. It also includes the ruins of a 17th century castle built as a part of the town's defences by Felipe IV. You can walk up to the hilltop from the Plaza de España or from Calle Camelias in town or drive and park outside the park.

The excavated area of the castro is on the eastern slopes of the hill where there are a group of circular and oval house foundations preserved. Also here are some reconstructed roundhouses, stone built with thatched rooves which give a good idea of what they would have been like. There is also a small interpretation centre and guided tours are available. The castro dates from the 3rd century BC into the Roman period, 3rd century AD.

The final site overlooks the Portuguese border, the River Miño and the Atlantic Ocean and is another castro must-see not least for these magnificent views.

Castro de Santa Trega

Castro unrestricted access
Museum restricted access

This site sits towards the top of Monte de Santa Trega, a granite hill of over 300m in height on the southern outskirts of A Guarda. The hill is easily accessible by car from the town with parking at various places on the way up. The top of the hill is a religious site with a church and the winding road up to it has statues and

Figure 4.24. Reconstructed houses at O Castro Vigo (Photo: Simon and Barbara Maddison)

the stations of the cross along its route. The castro was discovered in the 1920s when the road was being built resulting in the first archaeological excavations which have continued on and off since then.

Towards the top, on both sides of the road, are several extensively excavated and consolidated areas of excavation. The stone-built ramparts which enclose the hilltop are difficult to follow and the main interest is in the houses and internal layout of the site. There is a range of house types, mainly circular of which there about 100 excavated showing a continuing Iron Age influence through the Roman period of occupation. It is interesting how closely packed together they are with pathways between them. Some show details of hearths, thresholds and vestibules/porches, some stone door jambs and lintels show evidence of decoration with carved intertwined rope patterns and spirals. In places small groups of houses are clustered around a central courtyard perhaps representing an extended family unit. There is also evidence for drains beneath some of the floor slabs. There are reconstructed roundhouses with thatched rooves. The castro was first constructed in 400 BC and lasted until well into the Roman period, about AD 200, at its height it is estimated to have held 3,000 people.

As you walk around the excavations and other areas of the hilltop look out beneath your feet for petroglyphs, carved spirals and other designs on slabs of granite bedrock. These pre-date the castro by a long way being probably late Neolithic/early Bonze Age, about 2,000 BC. It is interesting to wonder whether the Iron Age castro builders were aware of these carvings and if so what they thought of them.

At the top of the hill, near the church, is a small museum which houses information on the castro and the findings of the excavations including Iron Age and Roman pottery and metal objects.

Figure 4.25. One of the excavated areas at Castro de Santa Trega (Photo: Simon and Barbara Maddison)

Around Logroño
La Rioja, Navarra
+ País Vasco
VITORIA-GASTEIZ
CASTILLA Y LEÓN
MIRANDA DE EBRO
PAÍS VASCO
CASTILLA Y LEÓN
NAVARRA
N
W
E
S
(I)
(I)
LAGUARDIA
LOGROÑO (M)
NÁJERA (M)
LA RIOJA
Dolmen
Castro
Settlement
(M) Museum
(I) Interpretation Centre

Chapter 5

Around Logroño: La Rioja, Navarra and País Vasco

Logroño is the capital of La Rioja and although there isn't a great deal to see there in terms of monuments (although the cathedral is wonderful) it is a nice place to relax either in town or in the park along the banks of the Río Ebro. Most people think of the obvious when Rioja is mentioned and this is certainly the place to partake, either by visiting the many bodegas in the area or by strolling around the old part of town and sampling the very good tapas bars which offer a boggling range of local wines together with some excellent tapas.

Museo de La Rioja, Logroño

Plaza San Agustín
Restricted access

Located in a very attractive 18th century palace just off Calle Portales, the main pedestrianised street which runs past the cathedral. The museum is recently (2014) opened after a major refurbishment and now offers very well presented and laid out collections with labelling in Spanish and English. There are a series of interactive audio-visuals (the interaction is not always obvious though!), and some very informative videos (with English sub-titles), for example one on prehistoric metal working.

The prehistoric material is on the first floor, rooms 2 to 4 with a good chronological presentation of local material and sites from the Palaeolithic period to the arrival of the Romans. The downside of Spanish political organisation, however, is shown by the fact that Logroño is located near the boundary of other autonomous regions and so nearby sites such as La Hoya and the megalithic tombs described below are not included even though they are just a few kilometres along the road – they are not in La Rioja.

Room 2 displays Palaeolithic, Neolithic, Chalcolithic and Late Bronze/Early Iron Age material of all sorts including some good pottery and domestic implements from the Iron Age defended site of El Redal with rectangular houses similar to La Hoya described below. Room 3 concentrates on the Celtiberians, the tribal groupings from the 5th century BC onwards with some very nice funerary stelae with engraved horses and goats. A video explains the importance of rotary motion to the Celtiberians as demonstrated through the use of the wheel, the potter's wheel and the rotary quern. Room 4 shows contact with Rome, 195-133 BC, the Roman conquest of the Ebro Valley and its impact on the indigenous people resulting in new cultural forms such as pottery, weapons and tools, and the use of money and writing.

Rooms 5 to 8 are an in depth look at all aspects of Roman life. The second floor of the museum covers the Visigoths from the 5th century AD and the Arab conquest of La Rioja from the 8th century. The third floor is a mixture of domestic and agricultural ethnographic material together with 19th and early 20th century art.

To the north and northwest of Logroño are a series of megalithic tombs (dolmen) plus the Iron Age settlement of La Hoya, many along the A124. The most accessible and best-preserved tombs are described below but if you only have time to see one let it be La Hechicera which has been excavated, restored and is well explained with a notice board.

The hilltop medieval walled town of Laguardia is beautiful and should be visited, there are many fine buildings and churches and the whole place has a calm and special feel. Before you start on the dolmen trail make sure you visit the local Iron Age settlement, the most important of its kind in the area:

La Hoya

Restricted access

Signposted from the A124 at Laguardia

This is a very important site for understanding later prehistoric life and death in this area. There is plenty to see in the on-site museum (although most of the displays are in Spanish and Basque only), you can then visit the excavations and finally walk around part of the original perimeter wall. The site was discovered in 1935 and the main excavations were between 1973 and 1989 although more work has been done recently including extensive geophysical survey. The settlement is of several phases, starting in the middle Bronze Age, then the late

Figure 5.1. The excavated area at La Hoya from the air

Bronze Age/early Iron Age (1200-450 BC) and finally in the middle Iron Age (450-250 BC) with a massive surrounding stone wall enclosing 4ha.

The evidence suggests that the settlement was attacked and destroyed around the mid-third century BC. Buildings were burnt to the ground and skeletons were found in the streets during the excavation. It seems that the settlement was not occupied again.

The museum explains the chronology, excavation methods together with agricultural and technological methods from the Bronze and Iron Ages. There are many artefacts, displays and audio-visuals. The highlight is the reconstructed large rectangular house with stone foundations, adobe, plank and wattle and daub walls, thatched roof showing daily activities such as weaving and food preparation going on inside.

Walking outside you can walk around an excavation trench which has been left open. This gives a good impression of the actual evidence in the ground and the density of the rectangular houses laid out with streets and pathways. Unfortunately, it has not been well maintained and the whole has an air of sad desolation about it.

Figure 5.2. A reconstruction of the houses within La Hoya

To see some of the original surrounding wall from the outside of the settlement, walk along the road left from the car park (the wall on your left may be on the original line but it is modern!). Where this swings left walk along the edge of the vines and on your left you will see some good stretches of original wall, in places up to 5m high.

Dolmen de La Cascaja

Unrestricted access

Starting furthest away from Laguardia and moving towards it, this is the westernmost of the group of tombs. From the A124 take the LR242 signposted to Peciña. About 1km before the village park in the church car park on the right, walk further along the road, the tomb is signposted off to the left along a track.

This is a circular stone cairn with a megalithic passage some two metres long leading into a single stone chamber. It has been excavated and reconstructed so the uprights and capping stones look good. The entrance through the passage faces the south-east which is common for these tombs. Within the chamber was excavated the human skulls and other selected bones that represented the remains of at least 31 individuals, deposited with animal bones and two broken pots all suggesting a Neolithic date. A bronze arrowhead was also found which may indicate that the tomb was late in the Neolithic and still being used in the early Bronze Age. These tombs were re-used, perhaps many times, with new bones being deposited over a period of time. The fact that only selected bones were deposited within the tomb suggests an initial funerary rite took place elsewhere, perhaps involving the de-fleshing of the bodies by exposure.

Figure 5.3. Dolmen de La Cascaja

Dolmen de Layaza

Unrestricted access

This is the most difficult one to find so if you are pressed for time it's the one to miss. Take the A2124 from the A124 west of Laguardia. Within the first kilometre after the turn, on the left just before the metal crash barrier starts on

Figure 5.4. Dolmen de Layaza

the side of the road, small stone posts indicate the way to the tomb about 50m from the road. The posts are difficult to see, the tomb is visible as a slight rise and definitely looks better close up.

This is a stone cairn about 12m in diameter and 2m high, the layout is typical of tombs in this area with a passage and single chamber at the end of it. The capstones have been removed. The location of this tomb is spectacular overlooking the plain of Rioja to the south with dramatic limestone cliffs to the north.

Dolmen El Sotillo

Unrestricted access

Continue along the A124 towards Laguardia, the tomb is well signposted from the road.

Another circular cairn with the top missing and the capstones, again a passage of which the uprights for about 3m survive leading to a single chamber. There appears to have been some restoration and there is a slight indication of a ditch around one side of the cairn.

Figure 5.5. Dolmen El Sotillo

Figure 5.6. Dolmen de San Martín

Dolmen de San Martín

Unrestricted access

Continue along the A124 towards Laguardia, the tomb is well signposted from the road.

Similar in form to the previous two but bigger and more impressive. The cairn has been partially rebuilt, about 8m of passage survive leading to the chamber although all but one of the capstones have been removed. Some of the stones are massively impressive.

Dolmen del Alto de la Huesera

Unrestricted access

Take the A3228 to Elvillar from the A124 at Laguardia. About 1.5km from the turn there is a house on the right with a swimming pool on a sharp bend, just after this on the opposite side of the road is a track which is tarmacked for the first 50m then gravel. The site is not signposted. Follow the gravel track to the top of the hill, the monument is on the right.

When we visited in August 2013 the site was being excavated, we haven't returned since. This is another circular cairn with passage and chamber. In the small car park to the side of the tomb are two large stones which may be original capstones, one has a curious 'basin' and water channel carved into it.

Figure 5.7. Dolmen del Alto de la Huesera

Dolmen de la Hechicera (La Chabola de la Hechicera)

Unrestricted access

Further along the A3228 towards Elvillar, before reaching the village the tomb is signposted from the road.

This is the best of the group as it has been excavated and restored plus there is a good information board in English. It is also in a spectacular location with good panoramic views, reinforcing the idea that these burial monuments were located to be seen from afar. The site was discovered in 1935 and has seen several phases of excavation. It was first constructed in the Neolithic, *c.* 3000 BC, and continued in use until the early Bronze Age, probably for 1,000 years or more. The circular cairn has been partially reconstructed to its original shape and size, as has the passage and the chamber although only a single capstone remains. At least 39 individuals were represented by a selection of bones together with arrowheads, beads and Bell Beaker pots from the early Bronze Age.

Figure 5.8. Dolmen de la Hechicera

Dolmen El Encinal

Unrestricted access

Carry on along the A3228 through the village of Elvillar in the direction of Kripan. Just through the village the site is signposted to the right along a track.

This is the same form, circular cairn, passage and single chamber with no capstones remaining.

Dolmen Los Llanos

Unrestricted access

Figure 5.9. Dolmen Los Llanos

Carry on along the A3228 towards Kripan, before reaching the village the site is signposted to the left.

This one is of a slightly different form to the others above. It still comprises a circular cairn with passage and single chamber, some of which is reconstructed although there are no capstones. As with some of the others, the cairn is surrounded by kerbstones but what's different here is that on the far side of the cairn (opposite the gate in the fence) the passage splays out to form a courtyard at the front of the entrance into the tomb. This type of feature is known elsewhere (in Ireland for example where they are called Courtyard Tombs) and it's thought that ceremonies and rituals would have been carried out here as part of the burial activities.

Dolmen Hipogeo de Longar (Longar Arazuri Hipogeo)

Unrestricted access

From the small town of Viana, north-east of Logroño on the N111, take the NA 7230, a small and spectacular road into the mountains towards Cabredo. Several kilometres out of town the site is signposted along a dirt track on the left. Drive for about 4.5km along this track, it is rough in places but the views are worth it. There is an initial display board about 1km before the tomb, a short length of concrete track, then park and walk.

The site has been excavated and reconstructed and there is a display board (in Spanish) with good detail of the excavations and the finds including skeletons with flint arrowheads embedded in them. The site dates to the late Neolithic, late Third Millennium BC. The tomb itself has been reconstructed and has a circular cairn with revetting stones, a passage with entrance courtyard and a raised step-stone at the entrance, leading to a single chamber. This tomb really emphasises the importance of location and shows the care taken in positioning these tombs as the entrance faces straight down the valley and a tremendous view.

Figure 5.10. Dolmen Hipogeo de Longar

South-west of Logroño

Situated 30k south-west of Logroño along the A12 is the small town of Nájera. Of great interest here is the Gothic Monasterio de Santa María la Real, particularly the 16th century cloisters. Inside are a fine collection of tombs of various kings of Castilla, León and Navarra together with beautifully carved choir stalls.

Nearby, a good local museum:

The Najerillense Museum, Nájera

Restricted access

Located in a delightfully restored medieval house, the former palace of the abbot of Santa María La Real close to the monastery (above) which should also be visited. In the old centre of the town of Nájera, best to park in the market square and walk over the river bridge into the old part of town where the museum is signposted.

The museum presents the archaeology of the Najerilla Valley from Palaeolithic times to the medieval period. The prehistory room is chronological and has good displays and distribution maps of sites and artefacts although it is all in Spanish. For example, around Nájera are 11 Celtiberian settlements, eight known from archaeology, one from 'history' and two from epigraphy with many artefacts on display including the curious and enigmatic decorated 'bloques prismáticos' and decorated funerary stelae showing horses and riders. There is nothing, or very little, to see of these sites on the ground and they are mostly known from surface finds which makes this display all the more important.

Further afield from Logroño: around Vitoria-Gasteiz

Castro de Henaio

Unrestricted access

This is just outside the village of Alegría-Dulantzi, about 15km east of Vitoria-Gasteiz, signposted from the village and on the A3110. There is a car park with an interpretation board, it's a walk of about 1km to reach the site.

There is a small interpretation centre (all in Spanish) with reconstructed roundhouses and although when we visited (August 2013) this was closed and in a bad state of repair, it is still worth a visit. The route around the site includes several interpretation boards, one describing the ramparts together with a length of reconstructed stone rampart and wooden palisade on the top. There are a series of levelled terraces where excavation revealed circular wattle and daub houses. On the top of the hill are three interpretation boards explaining points of interest in the views including historical sites. The location and landscape setting of this castro are impressive.

Figure 5.11. Reconstructed roundhouses at Castro de Henaio

The following are two dolmen east of Vitoria-Gasteiz, off the E5-E80.

Dolmen de Arrizala (Sorginetxe)

Unrestricted access

Approximately 35km from Vitoria-Gasteiz turn right into the village of Arrizala. Signposted as a right hand turn in the village onto a track into fields, then make sure you follow the tarmac track turning left (not signposted) to the site, not straight on.

The dolmen has a good chamber with five massive uprights and a single large capstone, no evidence for the cairn. The site has good views.

Figure 5.12. Dolmen de Arrizala

Figure 5.13. Dolmen de Aizkomendi

Dolmen de Aizkomendi

Unrestricted access

Just off the the E5-E80 left into the village of Eguílaz/Egilatz, well signposted through the village although a rather circuitous route.

This is another spectacular location with mountain views in the distance. There is an informative display board (in Spanish and Basque) explaining the excavation there and how the dolmen was built and used in the 5th and 4th millennia BC. The whole has been reconstructed so that the passage and chamber are visible within a cutaway mound which must have been massive originally and although the interpretation suggests that the passage splayed into a courtyard there is no evidence of this on the ground. Overall this site looks 'sanitised' for display and has an odd feel about it.

Castillo (and site of Castro) de Portilla

Unrestricted access

South of Vitoria-Gasteiz, in the village of Portilla, 20km north of Haro, follow the signs to the medieval Castillo along a footpath that goes up the mountain. This is a *c.* 30 minute walk which is steep in places. At the final sign (Castillo 50m) carry straight on to the recently cleared castle walls.

Exploring this area it isn't clear exactly what is related to the Castro although excavation has confirmed late Bronze Age and Iron Age occupation here. Within the castle walls are a series of levelled terraces which could be for occupation within the Castro and it is likely that the prehistoric evidence has been obliterated by the medieval activity. Even so, this is another chance to appreciate the spectacular location chosen for the Castro, and the castle is interesting. Of particular note is the unusual natural limestone 'wall' (a vertical bed of rock) which within the castle has been utilised to enclose an area with the built wall abutting up against it.

Nearby is the town of Miranda de Ebro just north of which are two dolmen:

Dolmen La Mina

Unrestricted access

Off the A625, 15km north west of Miranda de Ebro, the A4322 not far out of Molinilla towards Leciñana del Camino/Leziñana, take a dirt track on the left between fields (not signposted). The dolmen is a few hundred metres down this track in the field on the right surrounded by posts and a rope fence, visible from the track.

Figure 5.14. Dolmen La Mina

Figure 5.15. Dolmen La Lastra

The chamber and parts of the passage are visible although it is considerably damaged and there are no capstones. There are a lot of stones which suggest a massive covering cairn. A pile of spoil to one side of the chamber suggests it has been emptied. A nice location with good views.

Dolmen La Lastra

Unrestricted access

Continue from La Mina further down the same track, the dolmen is signposted to the right at a crossroads, positioned in a field.

Little of this survives although some upright stones indicate the chamber and there is cairn material around.

Aragón

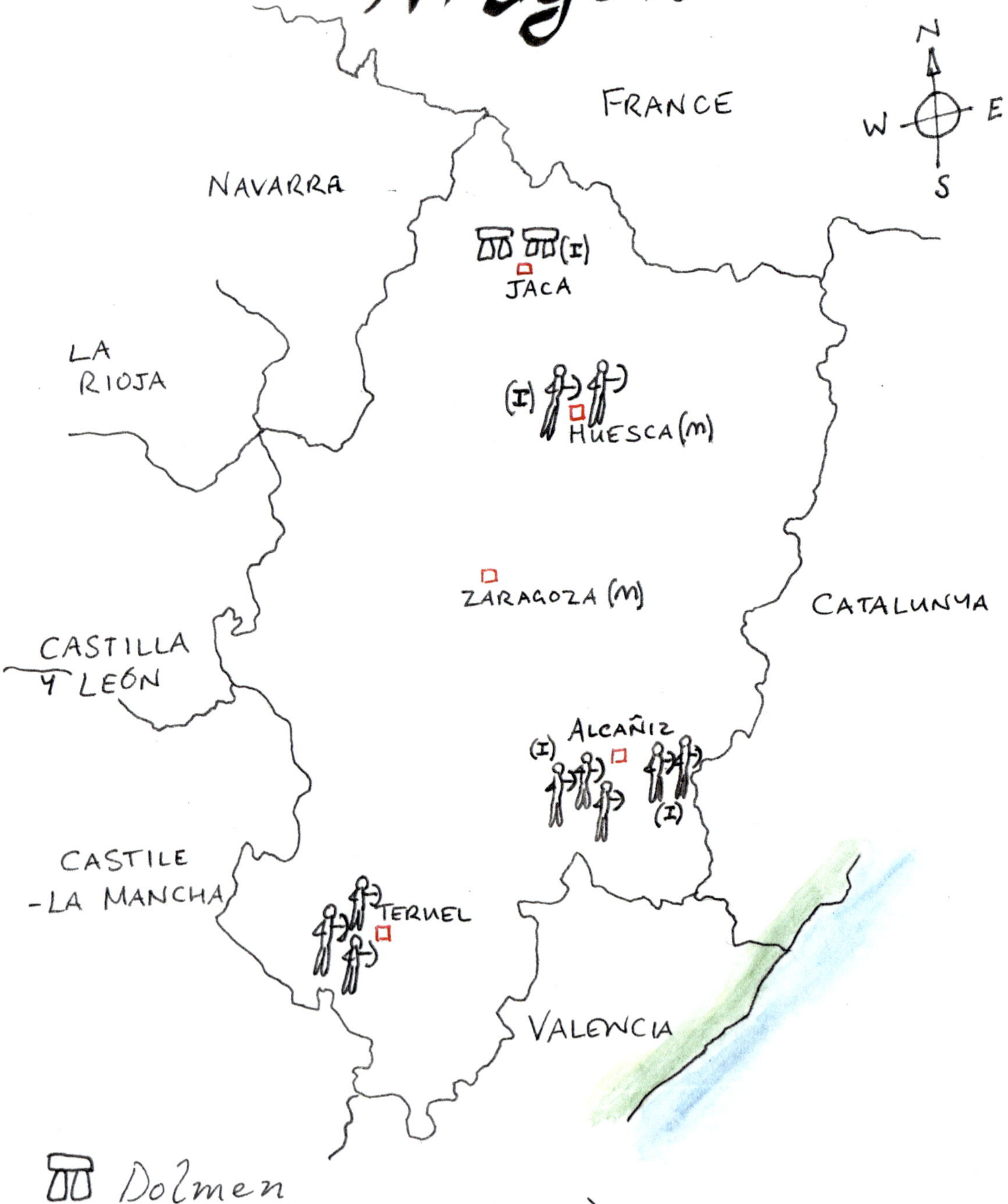

Dolmen
Rock Art (Rock Shelters)
(M) Museum
(I) Interpretation Centre

Chapter 6
Aragón

Rock art in Aragón

Along the Mediterranean seaboard of Spain is an exceptionally large collection of later prehistoric rock art (arte rupestre). This occurs in the Autonomous Communities of Andalusia, Aragón, Castile-la Mancha, Catalunya, Murcia and Valencia and numbers over 700 individual sites in total. The first art to be discovered was in Aragón where in 1903 a local man identified paintings at Roca dels Moros, near Cretas (see below). There are now 167 locations with art in Aragón and here we describe the few we have visited. Collectively these became a UNESCO World Heritage Site in 1998 under the heading of 'Rock Art of the Mediterranean Basin and the Iberian Peninsula'.

Within Aragón there are five main areas of art, all of which are sampled below:

Alto Aragón

Bajo Aragón

Alto Guadalope

Río Martín

Albarracín

Some of these have very good interpretation centres that provide a lot of detailed information on the art, the methods and techniques used, individual sites and explanations. Two good ones that we visited and would recommend are at Colungo (Alto Aragón) and Ariño (Río Martín). These also provide details of how to visit art sites, often with very good maps and leaflets. Generally speaking the directions to these sites are well signposted with *Arte Rupestre* signposts both on roads and walking paths. Some involve driving along a 'camino rural' which are un-surfaced tracks generally OK for ordinary cars although extremely dusty! Once you reach a site it will usually be enclosed by a metal grill (as in Figure 6.2) and there will be one or more interpretation panels (usually only in Spanish) which show the art of that site and the position of individual elements - its then up to you to spot it. At some sites it is very clear at others we found it impossible to see some of the figures.

To summarise some of the background detail:

This art is usually called Levantine Art, after this area of Spain, and is different in character and date to the Palaeolithic cave art of northern Spain (as described in Section 2 of this book). Typically, this art consists of paintings of human figures often carrying out daily tasks, often together with animals. These are important documentation of everyday life in prehistory, not only showing what people did and sometimes details of what they wore, but also what was important enough to them to want to record. Hunting activities are most frequently represented, often hunting by groups with details of animal traps and the tracking of wounded animals. Gathering activities, such as that of honey, are also shown. The earliest depictions of combats and executions appear in the form of archers shooting at their victims. Scenes of domestic daily life show groups of people sitting and talking, people walking together, seated hunters, and the butchering of animals. The representations of the human figures provide information on clothing, such as baggy trousers, and personal ornament including different hairstyles, head-dresses, bracelets, arm-rings and necklaces. It has been suggested that this variation in material culture shows an increasing social inequality. Funerary rites are depicted in the form of recumbent corpses and ritual scenes. Other scenes illustrate the mythologies of these prehistoric societies: sorcerers in strange costumes are common, as are figures combining human characteristics with those of animals (deer, bulls and birds). Female figures are also common, and these could represent female deities because of their prominent positions in the scenes depicted and their larger size. The art is usually painted in red and less often in black or even white, very occasionally there is some engraving. Individual elements can be quite small, 10cm or less, although some are much bigger. Some sites only contain one or two paintings while others contain whole friezes showing many different figures and animals and a range of activities. Some of these represent several periods of painting, the same site has been visited and painted many times as shown by later figures overlying earlier ones. The sites described below will not provide examples of all these aspects but will give a good feel for what this art is like.

Levantine art (arte Levantino) may have started in the Mesolithic period but is thought to be mainly Neolithic and, therefore, associated with the first farming communities dating to approximately 6,000 BC to 4,000 BC. A different style, Schematic art (arte esquemático), is found in the same areas, sometimes the same sites, and overlaps chronologically with Levantine art for about 1,000 years but lasts longer. This is probably associated with the first metal working societies and dates to the Chalcolithic Period, again approximately 3,500 BC to 2,000 BC. In Schematic art, as the name suggests, the naturalistic human and animal figures are replaced by much more enigmatic symbolic motifs, some are human-looking while others are geometric patterns and tree/fern-like symbols. The dating of both Levantine and Schematic art is contentious within Spanish archaeology and together they are sometimes referred to as 'post-Palaeolithic art' which is less problematic.

Note that the Palaeolithic art of northern Spain is much older, anywhere between 35,000 and 12,000 years ago and concentrates on animals rather than human figures. In Aragón there is only one known example of Palaeolithic art, the Cueva Fuente del Trucho (see Colungo below).

Another difference between Palaeolithic and Levantine art is in its location, and perhaps, therefore in the way it was intended to be seen and understood. The older art is in caves, often deep within caves suggesting that the viewing of it was in some way special and held a 'religious' meaning. Levantine art is nearly always in rock shelters (abrigos), usually in cliffs that look out over valleys, rivers, watery places, places where people would have lived, herded animals and perhaps farmed. This makes Levantine art much more open and accessible and perhaps indicates that it was more integrated into regular activities. The often expansive views over landscape may also be associated with a lifestyle which is changing from one of entirely hunting and gathering to one that includes agriculture, domesticated animals and a more sedentary focus.

This last point about location and landscape setting is important when visiting Levantine art. Sometimes this art is quite difficult to see, it is often small, painting in red ochre is the norm and this often fades, so once a site is reached it can be disappointing. But the location can make up for this! Some of the sites described below are in the most beautiful places and involve walks (sometimes quite long) through stunning landscapes to reach what are often remote places. For the sites described below, which we have visited, we try to give an indication of not only what there is to see when you get there but also the setting.

Museums

As with most Spanish cities and towns, and indeed many villages, the ones in the areas of Aragonese rock art have museums with archaeological collections. If it is the rock art that you are particularly interested in, however, the interpretation centres at the actual places of the art are much more informative (some of these are described below). We visited the following two museums and found them particularly enjoyable and informative, not least for the historic buildings that they are in. Of the two Huesca has the most interesting prehistoric collections.

Huesca museum

Restricted access

The 13th century cathedral of Huesca and the 16th century Town Hall, opposite, are both very attractive and interesting buildings at the centre of the old town. Especially fine is the decorated balcony of the Town Hall and the main doorway of the cathedral richly decorated with 14 figures on either side of the entrance. A five-minute walk from the Plaza de la Catedral is the museum located in an impressive 17th century Baroque octagonal old school building with a delightful courtyard. This is connected to the Romanesque 12th century Palace of the Aragonese Monarchs which is used for temporary displays.

The displays are well laid out in chronological order with labelling in Spanish only. The prehistoric collections are in Rooms 1 and 2 and include a good section on the Cueva de la Fuente del Trucho, the only Palaeolithic painted cave in Aragón, with detailed photographs and explanations of the painted and engraved horses, hands and dots. There is much material from excavated local sites and a good section on Levantine and Schematic rock art starting with a section on techniques and including a detailed account of the art in the Río Vero area. Of particular interest are the examples of this art in red ochre on stones and pebbles which are rare.

Room 2 moves on to the Chalcolithic and the Bronze Age with dolmen, evidence for bronze working and some very impressive large, decorated urns dating to 1250 BC to 1100 BC. There are also early Iron Age cremation burials, 650 BC to 350 BC, and some fine decorated pottery. Room 3 covers the Iberians, 350 BC to 50 BC, and the Romans and Room 4 the medieval period. The rest of the museum is devoted to art from the 13th century onwards with work by Goya and a good collection by the local 20th century artist Ramón Acín.

Zaragoza museum

Plaza de los Sitios
Restricted access

Located in another wonderful historic building, most of the archaeology collection is devoted to Zaragoza's origins as the Roman town of Caesar Augusta established in AD 14 on the banks of the River Ebro with a bridge over it. The collections are the result of many local excavations as well as historical references and are detailed and informative. The decorated iron chest in Room 8 is a highlight worth travelling to see.

The prehistoric collection is relatively limited and found in Room 10. It contains mainly late Bronze Age and Iron Age material, up to 18 BC when the Romans conquered this area. There are some unusual and important gems though including the Celtiberian head (Number 14) with very typical blank staring eyes (perhaps signifying death and this is the severed head of an enemy, a Celtic practice recorded by Roman writers). Also, the late Bronze Age, 900 BC, funerary stele with the carved notched shield design which is very typical for the period.

The second floor is devoted to art, mainly 19th and 20th century, with five rooms of Goya and two rooms of East Asian art.

Rock art sites

Alto Aragón -Río Vero

Your visit here should start with the *Centro de Arte Rupestre* (restricted access) in the village of Colungo, east of Huesca. From the N240 out of Huesca take the A129, left, through Adahuesca to Colungo, the Centre is signposted in the middle of the village where you can park. There are three elements to the Centre, the museum itself, an 'archaeological park' outside and a Fuente del Trucho cave room.

The ground floor of the museum is a general introduction to the River Vero area, its ecology, geology and the fact that since very earliest times it has provided an important route from the high Pyrenees to the valley of the River Ebro, the major river through north-eastern Spain to the Mediterranean. There are also informative displays (in Spanish but there is an English audio set available) on archaeological techniques and human evolution as well as details of the different types of art, Palaeolithic, Levantine and Schematic, and the materials and techniques used to produce them. On the 1st floor is a good video (available in English if you ask) and displays which show details of the art and sites in the area with examples of the main motifs.

Outside is the Archaeological Park which has reconstructions of Neolithic huts and a dolmen with an area for various types of demonstration, children were throwing spears when we were there. Apparently, the European Championship of Prehistoric Archery takes place here every two years but, unfortunately, it wasn't on when we visited. There is also a room devoted to the Fuente del Trucho cave, the only example of Palaeolithic cave art in Aragón. There are interesting displays showing the life of the people who lived in the cave and the art.

The first art in this area was discovered in 1968 and the area was made a Cultural Park in 2001, one of many in Spain, which means there is information available in the form of leaflets, maps and guides and signposts along routes. Good information is available from the museum on five sites that can be visited in the area (all unrestricted access), and at certain times of the year guided walks are available.

Figure 6.1. The Archaeological Park in the Centro de Arte Rupestre, Colungo

The two sites that we visited are along the A2205 Colungo to Ainsa road, from the parking area, both are signposted from the road. This is a beautiful drive along the Cañón del Río Vero, a dramatic steep-sided canyon with woodland and tremendous views. If you are only going to do one of these sites make it Tozal de Mallata as it has more visible art and the location is stunning.

Figure 6.2. Abrigo de Arpán showing a typical abrigo metal grill

Abrigo de Arpán

From the car park, about 9km from Colungo, it is a walk of approximately 40 minutes along the signposted track, the abrigo overlooks a ravine which is a tributary of the Vero. The Fuente del Trucho cave (see above) is not far from here but we were told at the museum it is not possible to visit. The art is quite difficult to see but there are red deer with antlers and on the left wall an archer with drawn bow and a possible scene showing a person gathering honey with a ladder all in black. Arpán typifies many of these sites in that the art is quite difficult to see but the location is beautiful making any visit worthwhile.

Figure 6.3. Abrigo de Arpán, a painted deer

Figure 6.4. Abrigos del Tozal de Mallata, human figures and a deer (© Clemens Schmillen)

Abrigos del Tozal de Mallata

Further along the road is the signposted parking place, it is an approximately 30-minute walk along the signposted track. There are two abrigos, both in towering limestone cliffs overlooking the rivers Vero and its tributary La Choca. The views over the karst landscape are tremendous with rows of caves and rock shelters visible in the cliffs. To reach these two involves some climbing using metal steps and walkways.

The art in both is Schematic, in Mallata 1, the first to be reached, are various scenes with humans some of whom appear to be roping deer by their snouts. There are also a series of red symbols, linear, circular and cruciform included. Further on is Mallata B, one of the most abundant art sites in the Río Vero. There are 13 people (some very hard to see), some with either head-dresses or big hair styles, again one is catching an animal by its snout with a rope. There are also symbols, again in red, especially a series of ramiform (branching) symbols.

Figure 6.5. Abrigos del Tozal de Mallata, ramiform symbols (© Clemens Schmillen)

Bajo Aragón

In this region we visited three areas with art, Cretas, Beceite and Valdealgorfa, all southeast of Alcañiz.

From the N420 out of Alcañiz take the A413 to Cretas. In the centre of the town take the road alongside the church signposted to Roca dels Moros y Gascons, the sites are 4km from here which is a very nice walk if you want to park in the town. The road turns into an un-metalled track, follow the red painted dashes. Look out for the modern rock art (don't be fooled!) – three deer painted on a rock face to the left of the road. Further on, a fenced area on the left-hand side is worth stopping at as it contains a reconstruction of a circular stone-built burial chamber dating to the 8th-5th centuries BC.

Abrigo de Roca dels Moros

The first site reached (signposted) contains two or three human figures and a small bull.

Abrigo Els Gascons

About 200m further along the track. The art is very difficult to see but contains a figure with a bow and arrow hunting.

These two sites were discovered in 1903 by a local amateur archaeologist and both show marks where art has 'disappeared', we are assuming it has been intentionally removed for display somewhere. This is supported by recording of the art in this area done by Cabré in 1915. Although the art is difficult to see at both sites the location is significant, they are low lying but overlook a small valley with a stream. This is an ideal place to live with animals even if the occupation is only for a short period of time and perhaps re-visited time and again. The art could mark the importance of this place and offer protection to those who camped there for a while.

Figure 6.6. Abrigo Els Gascons as recorded by Cabré in 1915

An aside – the Ruta Íberos en el Bajo Aragón

Although the Iberians are not included in this book as they are not strictly prehistoric, their archaeology is of great interest and includes many links with the prehistoric Celtiberians who lived at approximately the same time to the north. This Ruta offers 20 Iberian settlement sites and 11 small interpretation centres spread across a wide area centred on Alcañiz. One interpretation centre is in Cretas, go past the church and into a small street on the right before the square. Each centre has a different theme, in Cretas it is Iberian language and handwriting (there is also a small display of reproduced rock art from the two sites above). Here you can get information about the whole Iberian Route, the sites and centres.

Figure 6.7. Abrigo de La Fenellassa

Abrigo de La Fenellassa

To reach the small town of Beceite take the A2412 from Valderrobres. Once in the town follow the signs for 'El Parrissal' which is a popular walk along the valley of the Río Matarraña. The length of the walk is 6.5km each way, along the river through woodland, and is worth doing if you have the time. If not, there is a car park halfway along and you can walk the remaining 3km, or there is a car park at the end although access to this is restricted as it gets full. From this furthest car park follow the path to the rock art which is a little further on signposted to the right. Again, the location is significant as the art, three figures in red with some animals, looks out over a stream and grazing area.

La Val del Charco del Agua Amarga

Not far from Alcañiz, from the N232 to the southeast take the TE710 to the village of Valdealgorfa. As you enter the village (from the south) there is a signposted right turn with a rock art display board. Then turn left at the signpost and follow the signs, the road starts as concrete and here is a board with a phone number for a guide. A guide would enable you to get into the rock shelter which is fenced although you can visit and see the art from a few metres away without a guide. The road rapidly turns into a camino rural which you follow for *c.*10km through olive and almond groves.

This is an important site with over 150 paintings. It was discovered by the local pharmacist in 1913 and has recently been restored and conserved so visibility of some figures is very good. There are a range of human and animal figures of different sizes in red and black. Some humans have drawn bows, animals include deer and boar. On the right-hand side of the panel is a particularly good large red deer facing a small black deer.

Alto Guadalope - Castellote and Ladruñán

Start by visiting the Tourist Information Centre in the main square in Castellote which is on the A226, south off the main N211 south of Alcañiz. This area is the Cultural Park of Maestrazgo and the Tourist Office has a wealth of booklets and maps available including a guide book to the local rock art and a detailed map (ask the assistant to mark the best routes for you). Although in theory there are seven sites which can be visited around here we found it all quite confusing even with the help of the tourist information. We ended up just visiting two sites which are close together and involve a nice walk along a river. Be warned though, the river has to be crossed which might involve wading (depending on the time of the year).

Abrigos del Pudial (El Torico and El Arquero)

This is Ruta 1 in the tourist information guide book 'El arte rupestre de Castellote'. From Castellote take the road to Ladruñán, then to La Algecira where there is a small car park. Walk down to the river, turn left and follow the path along the river, there is an information board before you cross the river (no bridge) and follow the path.

El Torico is the first to be reached, difficult access but rewarded with a beautiful bull in dark red facing left.

Figure 6.8. Abrigo El Torico (© Comarca del Maestrazgo)

El Arquero has at least 23 figures although many are difficult to see. To the left are panels of Levantine art showing archers with bows and arrows, various other human figures, some female and a hunting scene where the victim is a male goat. All paintings are in red. There is also a panel of schematic art with arrangements of dots and motifs.

Río Martín

The best place to start here is:

The *Interpretation Centre in Ariño*, west of Alcañiz, from the A211 going south take the A223, then left on the small road, signposted. As you arrive in the village the interpretation centre is signposted on the right on the A1401 from the direction of Oliete. Although the landscape around here has been decimated by mining and isn't particularly attractive the wider area is the Cultural Park of the Río Martín and has many things of interest to see, not least rock art. This also means, of course, that maps, leaflets and guide books are available from the centre.

The centre has an excellent display that covers the main areas of rock art throughout Aragón, techniques and methods of rock art, many examples of figures and motifs and an animated film (ask for the English version) covering the life of the artists. In total there are 20 rock art sites that can be visited in this area, some involve a full day's walk and all are indicated, with access paths, on a free map. We visited the more accessible ones, the Barranco del Mortero and Tía Chula.

Figure 6.9. The Barranco del Mortero

Abrigo Barranco del Mortero

From Ariño take the A1401 towards Oliete and Muniesa, turn right after Oliete to Alacón. On the northern outskirts of town take the Carretera de las Ventas which after a short distance is signposted straight on to 'Mortero' and right to 'Ermita and Cerro Felio'. Both rock art sites are in the barranco (a dry valley) and you can park at one and walk to the other (probably about a *c.* 10km round trip).

We visited Mortero first by car, then returned for Cerro Felio. Continue straight on for about 5km, the car park for Mortero is on the right and signposted. Follow the path down into the valley. Behind the grill on the left there is a group of human figures which are reasonably clear and others which are very difficult to see. We struggled to make out any paintings behind the second grill which is a short walk across the valley.

Abrigo Tía Chula

Either walk along the valley, or drive back to the junction, turn past the ermita and follow the camino rural to the signposted car park. From here follow the red-topped posts along the path which winds its way up to the cliff face. Warning – there are a series of rock shelters here spaced along the cliff face and quite high up. The path goes to these in a circular route so that you eventually end up back near the car park. Parts of this path are very steep and quite precarious as it snakes along the cliff face and it is not for the feint hearted or anyone worried by heights. The art, as ever, is variable in quantity and quality but does include all of the main characteristics of both the Levantine and Schematic repertoires: individuals and panels, red and black.

Again the location and landscape setting are significant with all of the rock shelters and their art looking out over the valley which may have had a stream in it and would have been a perfect place for temporary settlement.

Frontón de la Tía Chula

In Oliete where the main A1401 crosses the river a small road follows the Río Martín (over the bridge immediately on the right if approaching from Alacón). This is a nice short drive along the river and after a few kilometres there is a sign-posted path to the left. As you approach the site there is a bench and an information board which suggests that certain 'solar alignments' from this location and involving the rock art site were significant in prehistoric times. It is certainly a bench with tremendous views where you can appreciate the landscape around the hilltop town of Oliete, the fertile valley bottom, the terraced hillslopes and the baron hilltops. The art is of the Schematic type and includes various wavy line motifs and at least one good figure.

Figure 6.10. Frontón de la Tía Chula (© Rosa Pérez)

Albarracín

This large group of rock art sites are on the outskirts of Albarracín, west of Teruel along the A1512. On the eastern side of town take the small road to Bezas, sign posted for rock art, all of the sites are along here on the left-hand side. This is probably the most rewarding group of sites to visit. You can do them all in a day and it involves a lovely well sign-posted walk through a pine forest. The art is tremendous with some exceptional examples of figures, animals and panels. In this area there is a total of 26 rock art sites that can be visited, we did the following in a day (all unrestricted access):

At the first car park, signposted for the Fuente del Cabrerizo, park and follow the signs down into the ravine, turn left and follow the arrows.

Fuente del Cabrerizo

Here there are two engravings, unusual as paintings are the norm, a deer to the left and a horse to the right. The horse is the clearest (on the flat surface above the board) and has its body infilled with pecking which, again, is unusual.

Figure 6.11. Fuente del Cabrerizo

Figure 6.12. Abrigo de los Cazadores del Navazo (© Falconaumanni)

Retrace your steps and then follow the S1 path to Del Navazo where there are four sites, signposted along the GR10 and then left. This is a beautiful walk through sandstone rock outcrops and pine forest. The next two sites are signposted:

Abrigo de Lázaro

Two scenes of red paintings in hollows in the rock face above the sign. In the lower scene are two archers, one of them very well preserved, in the upper scene an archer and some form of quadruped animal.

Abrigo de los Cazadores del Navazo

Here there are three engraved figures, all clearly visible. They hold a range of equipment including a possible bow, the one on the left appears to be holding a tree-like thing, the middle and left figures have shields.

Follow the signs to the next two sites:

Abrigo de los Toros del Prado del Navazo

This is an amazing site, the most important in the Albarracín area – if you only see one rock art site make sure it is this one! This was the first site in the area to be discovered, in 1892, and it is easy to see why as it is very accessible, and the art is very clear. It comprises a panel of 19 elements approximately 4.2m long and 1.4m high. The most striking aspect is the frieze of 9 bulls of different sizes but some of them the largest compositions in any Levantine art. There is also a horse, some

Figure 6.13. Abrigo de los Toros del Prado del Navazo

indeterminate quadrupeds and five archers. All the paintings are white and the bulls are infilled with white, except for one archer and one bull which are black. The archers are line paintings and the black one is particularly clear.

Carry on to the nearby:

Abrigo de Tío Campano

This has red paintings of deer, a horse that appears to be tethered and a human figure. The panel was probably bigger originally as there is some damage to the rock surface.

Return along the main path to the junction. Here you can either turn right to retrace your footsteps to the first car park and then drive along the road to the second car park, or you can turn left to visit the remaining sites and then walk back to the first car park. The second car park has a picnic area and a small interpretation centre (restricted access and closed when we visited).

From the second car park follow the signs to the Zona del Arrastradero, along the S2 path, this is a circular route:

Abrigo de la Cocinilla del Obispo

Here is an impressive panel of eight bulls facing both ways, 5.7m long in total, all white except for one black one. The one on the right has a very clear head and horns. There is also a horse and other figures but they aren't very clear.

Abrigo del Arquero de los Callejones Cerrados

The most impressive figure here is a dark red/black archer lying face down perhaps swimming or preparing to take aim with his bow while hiding. He is male as shown by a penis. This figure is the logo of the Parque Cultural de Albarracín. There are other human and animal figures but they are very faded and in white.

Just to the right of this abrigo is a reconstructed hut, the Chozo de Resineros, which shows how the rock art users may have lived. Follow the signs to the Mirador, about another 100m, for wonderful views across the landscape. Retrace your steps and continue around the loop signposted 'Pinturas'.

Figure 6.14. Abrigo del Arquero de los Callejones Cerrados

Abrigo de los Dos Caballos

Five animal figures in red, including a boar. The large central horse is the clearest.

Abrigo del Medio Caballo

Horse, bulls and a group of deer plus human figures with goats, in red and black. They are not all clear although a small red horse is visible on the right and two black bulls on the left of which the right hand one is clear. To the left is a small panel of schematic art showing spirals created by 'pecking' the rock face.

Abrigo del Ciervo

Poorly preserved and not very clear are a deer and bovine in red.

Abrigo de las Figuras Diversas

Here you can see a black bull facing right and just above it a deer in red with antlers also facing right. To the left is a strange human figure, very long and thin. We noticed that these figures were much more visible when the sun shone directly on them at about mid-day

These last three sites, which are close together, all overlook a flat area that would be ideal for a temporary settlement and for herding animals.

Figure 6.15. Abrigo de Doña Clotilde

Return to the car park and about 1k further along the road is a signpost for the next abrigo (it is well worth doing this final one as it has very interesting figures):

Abrigo de Doña Clotilde

An important group of at least 43 figures including 15 animals and 19 humans. There are also various schematic symbols and shapes. In red and black. There are two particularly good archers with bows and head-dresses, and in total at least six figures appear to have head-dresses or intricate hair styles.

Back on the road are signposts to the Interpretation Centre at Dornaque (10k further on), this is to do with forestry and ecology not archaeology.

Our second area in Aragón is to visit megalithic tombs, dolmen, in the north of the region, just west of the town of Jaca.

Valle de Hecho/Val d'Echo

This beautiful and spectacular valley of the Río Aragón Subordán runs up into the foothills of the Pyrenees, ending very close to the French border. The upper reaches, from Selva de Oza onwards, contain one of the densest distributions of dolmen anywhere in Spain with over 140 having been identified. Having said that, the majority are hard to find due to their poor condition, the fact that they are quite small and that there are many confusing natural boulders strewn across the landscape. The information provided below divides the upper valley into three areas each of which provides a good half day walk with dolmen being relatively easy to find; around Selva de Oza, the middle valley and the upper valley. The middle and upper regions are above the tree line and provide open summer mountain pasture for cattle, sheep and goats, which are moved to lower areas in the winter. Today's practice of transhumance is a continuation from middle Bronze Age times, approximately 1,500 BC, when it is first identified in the archaeological record through the appearance of specialist herders alongside the mixed farming practices, which started in the Neolithic. Rather than moving the animals on foot as in prehistory, these days during late September and October the mountain tracks are alive with small trailers full of animals.

We travelled in the area in early to mid-September and were lucky with the weather. The views to the surrounding high mountains are spectacular and the prevailing sound of cow and goat bells is very enigmatic in the high valleys. The animals are well cared for and give no problem even those with new calves. A small herd of horses mingled in the middle valley and protected their foal but presented no problems to walkers.

The road along the valley is the A176 and the mountain town of Hecho is well worth a stop on your way through and a wander around its picturesque narrow streets. The houses are rather sombre built from large blocks of local stone and one unusual feature is the circular, sometimes very wide and high chimneys. According to local information these need to be higher than the steep roof ridges to carry away the smoke from the ovens and hearths below. In the 9th century Hecho was briefly the seat of Aragonese power.

From Hecho take the narrow HUV2131 through the small village of Siresa with its very impressive 11th century church, once one of the earliest monasteries in Aragón which housed the biggest library in Spain. Continue along the ever-narrowing road until the Megalithic Interpretation Centre on the right-hand side in a converted forestry building.

The Megalithic Interpretation Centre

Restricted access

When we visited the man in charge spoke English and was very happy to talk megaliths. Here you can get a map of the valley with the main groups of megaliths shown.

Downstairs is a bar/café. Upstairs there are two display rooms and a small audio-visual room where you first watch a short film (there is an English version if you ask for it). This is a run through the history of the valley from prehistoric times to the present day.

In the summer months there are guided walks along the Camping Selva de Oza route (described below), information, times and booking at the Centre.

Display Room 1 has a general account of prehistoric developments from the Neolithic to Iron Age periods. It is well presented with artefacts, many images and text (in Spanish only). The transition to the Neolithic is explained with panels on cereal growing, bone tools, basketry, pottery and other aspects of life crucial to the change from hunter gatherers to sedentary farmers. Special focus is given to farming and animal domestication and herding which are particularly relevant to the valley. There is also a display on the interesting site of Corona de los Muertos, which is easy to visit, see below.

Display Room 2 is devoted to megalithic monuments and gives good detail of the different types, their construction and possible meanings to the people who built and used them. The main types, all present in the valley, are dolmen (communal burial chambers), menhirs (single standing stones), barrows (usually single burials) and stone circles (often called cromlechs). Very few of the valley dolmen and barrows have produced burials probably due to being robbed. The mapping of the valley megaliths has shown that they tend to occur in groups, often on hillocks or higher visible places. The possible reasons for this are discussed suggesting that they could be route markers for people moving along the valley, and/or indicating land ownership by different groups of people. It has been noticed that many of the dolmen have a chamber facing east, which may suggest sun worship. The first three types of monument are Neolithic in date whereas cromlechs started in the early Bronze Age, around 2,000 BC, some with barrow-like mounds in their centre.

Carry on along the road until on the left you reach Camping Selva de Oza. This is the last of the campsites on offer in this rather remote area and well worth a stay. It has recently reopened after being abandoned for over 30 years and the rebuild of amenities, including rooms to rent is of a high standard. It is very close to all the remains and so an excellent starting point.

Selva de Oza, circular walk

Unrestricted access

This easy circular walk takes a maximum of two hours and goes through woodland with high mountain views.

Within the campsite, around the back of the bar/restaurant is a dolmen. It's not well preserved but part of the cairn can still be seen together with three large stones, uprights and a possible capstone of the chamber.

Opposite the campsite take the track signposted to Camino a Espata (also to Corona de Los Muertos). After a few hundred metres take the signed path to the left, follow it through the woods to the:

Corona de Los Muertos

This interesting site in the woods, consists of a series of circles of stones, the best preserved are within fenced areas, the first two of which are close together and have an information board (in Spanish). Excavation of at least two of these circles has dated them to the period between the late Neolithic and early Iron Age (*c.* 3,000 BC to 500 BC). This very wide date range seems to match the uncertainty surrounding the function of these monuments and the site as a whole is claimed to span from 7,000 BC to the medieval period. The excavated circles seem to be the remains of simple roundhouses with structural postholes and hearths, perhaps temporary stopping places for animal herders moving around the valley. The confusion may arise as these look very similar to chromlechs (small stone circles with funerary and ritual purposes). From the excavations there are late Neolithic and early Bronze Age flint tools but also medieval iron weapons including a spearhead. Follow the path down to the third fenced area, which encloses one of the best circles, and then to the large fourth area which has many more. In the woods around this area it is possible to see more circular settings of stones. The board suggests that there are around 120 circles in this area and they may not have had a single function over the long time span of their use. From a non-archaeological view point we were told it is like being in the midst of numerous mystical fairy circles.

Figure 6.16. Corona de Los Muertos

Retrace your steps back to the main track, turn left and continue along it. After a kilometre or so take the signed path on the right, to Oza, down a steep slope through the woods. Follow the path and the signs (the GR11 path) until you reach a 'Go Ape' type of playground on your right. Go through this and at the other side is a board (in Spanish) for the dolmen:

Dolmen de Ramiro El Monje

The whole thing is not in good condition but the remains of a once impressive cairn can be seen by the number of water worn stones around the surviving standing stones. A large circular setting of stones can be made out and followed around the remains of the central chamber, now just two or three large stones which don't make much sense. There are large shallow hollows which suggest past digging into the central area. The interpretation board suggests a date of 3,000 BC to 1,500 BC, late Neolithic to early Bronze Age, and that the dolmen itself originally stood on the top of the cairn but if so this would have been very unusual. It is more likely that the cairn covered the uprights of the chamber and just the capping stone(s) were visible. The positioning of this dolmen is impressive on a high point overlooking the river and its valley, an auspicious place to be buried.

Cross the river to the road, turn right and return to the campsite.

The middle valley area

Unrestricted access

Continue along the road from the camp site until reaching the first car park and picnic area on the left, park here. Walk across the bridge over the river, this walk follows the GR11 long distance walking path through spectacular scenery and runs parallel to the road and the river for much of the way.

Figure 6.17. Dolmen de Puente de los Troncos

Immediately over the bridge, on the left and about 30 metres up the slope is a dolmen called the *Puente de los Troncos* although it isn't named. There are two parallel stones of the chamber about 0.4m above ground and with a small shrub in the middle of them, scattered stones nearby may be the remains of the cairn. This is an example of a poorly preserved and difficult to find megalith typical of this valley but don't be despondent if you can't find it as the others described below are all more obvious.

Carry on along the GR11 for about 15 minutes until a small bridge and a display board with information on dolmens. A further board also gives information about the route being known as the Le Chemin de la Liberte. Whether this was named for the Spanish Republicans fleeing to France at the end of the Civil War or for the French resistance going into Spain it was the road used since Roman times.

Here you can turn left upslope and walk to the two *dolmen of Acherito and Ferrias* although we didn't visit these. Just over the bridge on a small mound to the left is the *Casa de la Mina* dolmen with capstones, uprights and much cairn material scattered around. This is typical of the valley dolmen in being located on a slightly raised area overlooking the river.

Further along the GR11 is a refugio on the left, about 15 minutes, from here the track becomes a path but is still the GR11. Continue for about another 10 minutes and on the left is the *Dolmen de Barranco del Arroyo*, again there is not a board so it isn't named. As with some other monuments in the valley a low wooden post in the ground close to the path indicates it. There are three good uprights of the chamber *c.*1m tall and a considerable amount of cairn material showing a circular shape.

Figure 6.18. Dolmen de Barranco del Arroyo

About 25 metres upslope from the dolmen and path is a chromlech (burial mound), possibly two or three conjoined. Again on a slight hillock there are several sections of set stones, up to 0.5m high, forming parts of circles.

Carry on along the GR11 for about 30 minutes and you reach the *Las Fitas* group, again no board so not named. Close to the path three low circular posts mark the sites. The first is a stone circle with a single stone *c.* 1.5m high and others of 0.5m maximum. The centre shows a large hollow, which is probably the result of grave robbing. The next site, not far away, is a dolmen with three or four large uprights and other stones. The third site, just off the hillock and by the path, is a badly damaged dolmen with at least three uprights still in place and several other large stones nearby. Upslope from the group is a poorly preserved dolmen, unmarked but with one upright and several other large stones. Again, the positioning of this group on relatively high ground overlooking the river is typical of these valley monuments and obviously carefully chosen.

From here you can return to the car park or continue along the GR11. According to the map from the Interpretation Centre there is another group of dolmen further along the path, the Mallo Blanco group, although we didn't visit them.

Figure 6.19. El Salto

The upper valley

Unrestricted access

This is about a three-hour return trip walking to take in a barrow and a dolmen (with others optional) through spectacular scenery, alternatively you can drive some of the way.

Take the road from Selva de Oza, past the first car park as above all the way to the second car park, the road turns into a track before this and is rough in places although accessible by car. Park here and continue on foot along the track. After about a 45 minute walk there is a signpost on the left to Guarrinza La Mina, follow the footpath for about 20 metres to the *El Salto* barrow (not named). The barrow is visible on the left, from the main track, as a circular cairn of stones.

Continue along the track or take the marked GR11 path, which is a short cut and goes to the left after the bend, a stiff walk but safe enough, either way they bring you to a small refugio. The path gets thinner here and you need to go left upslope immediately after the refugio, follow the hillside around and then down into the valley.

Dolmen Aguas Tuertas is about ten minutes from the refugio, has an information board which is visible as you descend towards it. This is one of the best dolmen in the valley with a well preserved chamber, uprights, capping stone and cairn material as well as being situated in a position overlooking the beautiful mountain transhumance pastures of the upper valley. From here you can continue through the valley where there are more dolmen, according to the Interpretation Centre map, or, as we did, return to the car park along the same route.

Figure 6.20. Dolmen Aguas Tuertas

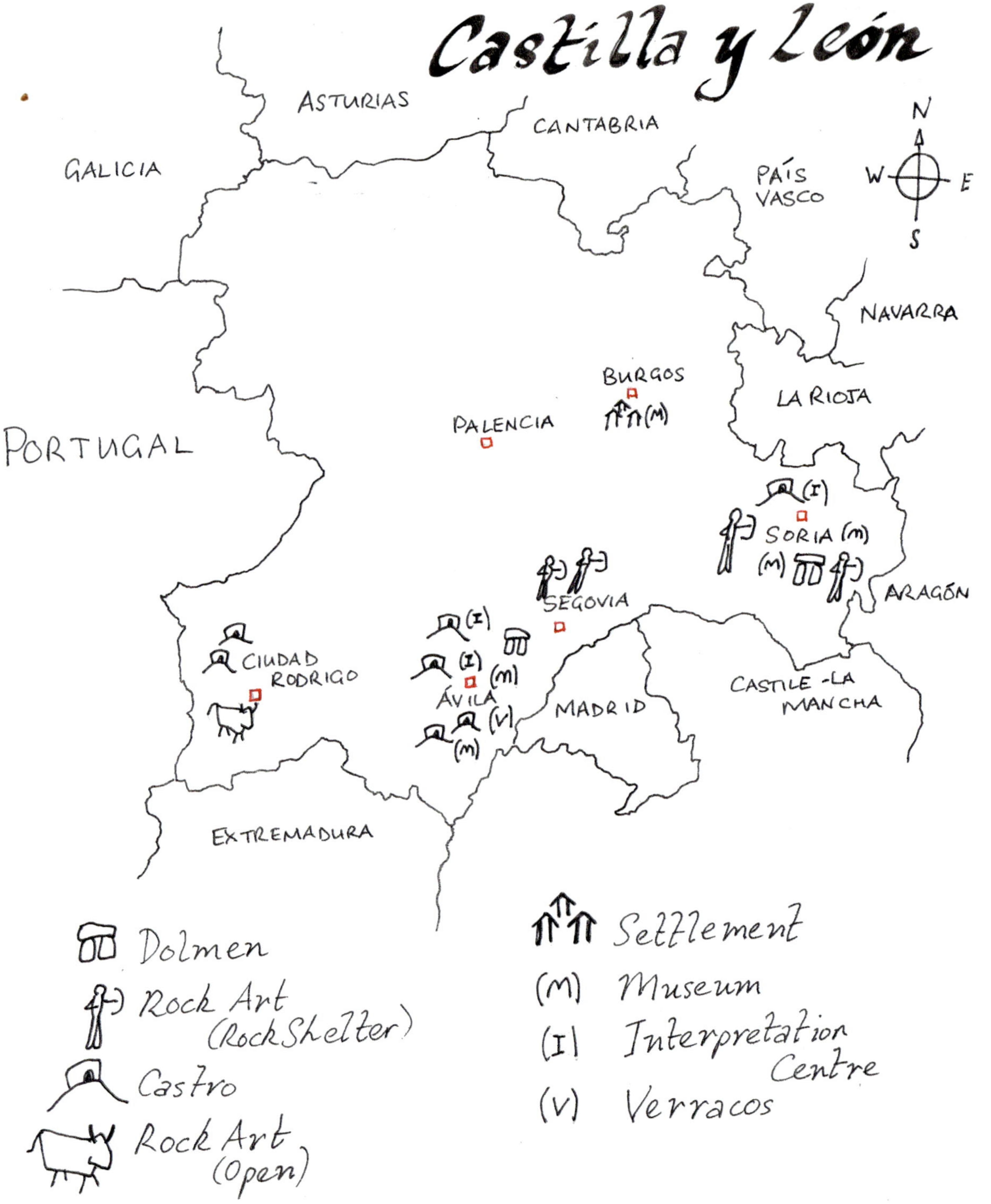
Castilla y León
ASTURIAS
CANTABRIA
GALICIA
PAÍS VASCO
N
W
E
S
NAVARRA
BURGOS
LA RIOJA
PALENCIA
(M)
PORTUGAL
(I)
SORIA
(M)
(M)
SEGOVIA
ARAGÓN
(I)
CIUDAD RODRIGO
(I)
(M)
ÁVILA
(V)
MADRID
CASTILE -LA MANCHA
(M)
EXTREMADURA
Dolmen
Rock Art (Rock Shelter)
Castro
Rock Art (Open)
Settlement
(M) Museum
(I) Interpretation Centre
(V) Verracos

Chapter 7
Castilla y León

This large region of central Spain is characterised by extensive flat plains, the central meseta, and beautiful mountain ranges such as the little-known Sierra de Francia with its distinctive villages of timber and stone buildings. The main cities all have historic features which need to be seen to be believed – the Renaissance architecture of Salamanca, the Roman aqueduct of Segovia, the cathedrals of León and Burgos which are amongst the finest in Europe and the stunning medieval town walls of Ávila. Spaniards sometimes describe the climate of the central meseta as 'nine months of winter and three months of hell' – it does get very cold and very hot!

Here we cover a selection of the prehistoric archaeology of the region, starting in the west and moving eastwards. Some of the sites described here are late Bronze Age/Iron Age/Roman defended settlements and there is a certain amount of confusion over what they are called. Many are known in this area as oppida, a term also used over much of Europe while further north in Spain the equivalent sort of sites are called castros although some in this area are so called as well. In the UK they are hillforts. It has been suggested that oppida may be later than castros/hillforts and also are generally bigger. The names we use here are those we found to be used locally.

Associated with oppida/castros are two features which are more common in this area than elsewhere in Spain, verracos and piedras hincadas:

Verracos are Iron Age carved stone statues, usually of stylised bulls and pigs (or boars), that stand about 1m high and up to 2.5m long (see page 126). Some have been re-located to their present positions and were probably originally carefully placed in the landscape or stood at the entrances to castros. This location near entrances has suggested that they were of symbolic/sacred importance to impress people entering the settlement although their function has been much debated. They were first recorded in the 16th century with an inventory of 63 and now there are about 400 known in total. Their distribution correlates approximately with the area of the western meseta occupied by the *Vettones*, the local pre-Roman tribe. The oldest verracos date to the 4th century BC and could have developed from 5th century Iberian statues. They stop being produced in the mid-2nd century BC when the Romans arrived and the social structure of the area changed with some castros being abandoned and others becoming 'Romanised'. After the Roman conquest smaller but similar carvings were used as decoration on funerary monuments.

It is of interest to mention here a detailed study of verracos in the Amblés Valley, to the west of Ávila where the three castros described below are located, Los Cogotas, La Mesa de Miranda and Ulaca. The castros are on the higher valley sides while in the lower areas there are contemporary undefended settlements. Here there are 70 verracos, the small number associated with the castros are positioned at animal enclosures while the majority are in the lower valley where they are correlated with good pasture lands, woodland and water sources. These are resources essential for cattle and pigs and, it is argued, as these represent the wealth of the *Vettones* so the verracos are symbolic markers of that wealth and the associated control of the resources. This may also suggest transhumance with the animals being moved to higher pastures in the summer while the lower, winter, resources were more in demand. This process still happens today with the 'alpaje' being the annual 'upward journey'. The archaeological evidence from the three castros, especially the grave goods from the many cremation graves in associated necropoli, suggests an increasingly stratified society so perhaps we are seeing a 'livestock elite' controlling areas of land and living in the castros.

Piedras hincadas (upright stones), (see Figure 3.13). In the UK these are known by the French name *chevaux de frise* although this is misleading as they are not the same as the 16th century defensive structures used by the Frisians to prevent cavalry attacks. Piedras hincadas are rows of upright stones embedded in the ground usually in groups in front of the defensive walls or around the entrances to oppida/castros/hillforts. Excavation has suggested that wooden stakes may also have been used. The usual interpretation of these is as a defensive measure to hinder attackers and force them towards more defensible areas of the walls. Their function and origin have been much discussed and they could also be partly symbolic to show the strength of the resident group. They are known mainly from Scotland, Wales, Ireland and Portugal with very occasional examples elsewhere. There are 86 sites in the Iberian peninsula with piedras hincadas of which 70 are in the north west, in Spain concentrating on the northern meseta. Recent radiocarbon dates from excavations around some piedras hincadas date their origin to the late Bronze Age, the 8th century BC, and they probably continued in use through the Iron Age.

Around Ciudad Rodrigo

Arte Rupestre de Siega Verde

Restricted access

Rock carvings from the Palaeolithic period are relatively rare and only recently recognised, here the first one was discovered in 1988 by a shepherd. They are an 'outdoor version' of cave art with representations of animals, mainly horses and aurochs, inscribed and pecked onto natural outcrops of rock along river valleys, it is not known whether they were originally coloured as some cave art is. Siega Verde is the main concentration in Spain and if you are really interested in this, and have a day to spare, it is worth going over the border into northern Portugal to visit Foz Côa, about 85km away, the main centre for this art where a much bigger selection is on display along the valley of the River Côa (together with a large, impressive museum dedicated to the Palaeolithic period and its art).

Siega Verde is on the DSA-470, 2km from Serranillo (north-west of Ciudad Rodrigo along the SA-324), where the road crosses the River Águeda (which flows into the Douro as does the Côa), park at the Interpretation Centre, the rusty-looking building. This contains an interesting display on the Palaeolithic period and it is worth watching the film (available in English) which is informative if rather over-sentimentalised. It is also worth buying the guide book which has line drawings of the art panels as it can be difficult to see some of the originals *in situ*. The oldest carvings here date to *c.* 18,000 BC, towards the end of the last Ice Age, the dating of them is based on stylistic comparisons with cave art. It is thought that here the pecked forms are earlier than the incised carvings.

Tours are led by a guide and the normal tour includes five panels of art on vertical(ish) faces of schist (if you ask you may be able to do the 'full tour' of 14 panels). In total here there are over 500 figures on over 90 panels but they stretch over 1.5km of the river bank and most can not be visited, there are also display boards (in Spanish). As at Côa, the tour takes you along the edge of the river and it is important to remember that the water level in the Palaeolithic was probably very different, here in fact five 'beach lines' have been recognised all higher than the current river and it is likely that with the melting of the ice sheets flooding would have been a regular event. The occurrence of art in the river valleys could show the importance of these places for humans encountering animals, perhaps hunting them at watering spots, also perhaps as humans used the rivers as routes for movement. As with cave art, a possible interpretation of these representations is related to hunting, both thanking the deities and encouraging a future supply, although it does seem that many of the species represented in the art were not hunted based on comparisons with bone assemblages excavated at camp sites and in the mouths of caves. Survey and excavation at Côa have identified camp sites with hearths and various stone tools although evidence of structures is rare.

Figre 7.1. Engravings at Siega Verde

Horses are the commonest here although other species include exotics such as rhino and bison. Panel 5 (just before going under the bridge) is one of the most interesting with an auroch almost 1m long, a small wolf, two small horses and a goat's head and horns (thought to be looking at you). Also on this panel are two recent circles (graffiti?) which stand out as being white, the fresh face of the rock, and show that when originally carved in the Palaeolithic the other figures would have been as visible and distinctive.

North of Siega Verde are three castros, all very accessible and interesting. Take the SA324 north to the town of Lumbrales. About 11km before Lumbrales at San Felices de los Gallegos, is a verraco just off the road by an old church. Around the back of the church, in the cemetery wall above the grilled window, is a carved head, possible Celtic.

Castro de Las Merchanas

Unrestricted access

This site is located not far from Lumbrales, from the centre of which it is signposted westwards along the CL-517. This single track road runs through countryside for about 7km until reaching the car park indicated by a piece of iron art work. The path to the site is well signposted and about 500m long, just before the castro is a restored water mill (put your hands through the iron grill on the door and wait for a surprise!).

Figure 7.2. Castro de Las Merchanas

The castro itself has good, new display boards (in 2012) and the recommended route starts at the inturned entrance, Iron Age with Roman alterations, the substantial walls were initially constructed in the 2nd/1st centuries BC. Follow the path through the interior of the castro to the other inturned entrance at the east, notice the track is cut down through the bedrock inside the entrance, this is probably Iron Age. Outside this entrance is a verraco boar and a very good example of a 'campo de piedras hincadas' (a field of chevaux de frise), best viewed from the top of the wall, you can climb up from the inside.

The two other things worth seeing here are the length of Roman walling in the interior which is probably part of a public building as statues were found during excavations there. Also, the Iron Age rock carving known as El Ferrari, so named by the locals as it looks like a racing car. This is reached through the small gate opposite the eastern gate, follow the small path around to the right, the carving is on the outside of the castro wall, there is a display board there.

Having visited the castro it is worth going back into Lumbrales to the museum (restricted access) which is in Plaza Mayor, the very attractive columned building which used to be the town jailhouse. On the way through town look out for the verraco on a small traffic island at a road junction. The museum has a collection of over 6,000 artefacts all collected and donated by local people, from the Palaeolithic to Roman periods. It also has a lot of material, artefacts, photographs and explanations, relating to the excavations at the Castro de Las Merchanas. Around the corner from the Plaza Mayor, the square outside the large church, is a verraco (not easy to tell what animal it is) and the Centro de Visitantes (restricted access), a new museum with some prehistoric material in it.

Castro de Yecla la Vieja

Unrestricted access

About 20k east of Lumbrales along the CL517 take the DSA453/450 past Yecla de Yeltes towards Villavieja de Yecla. Approximately 1km past Yecla de Yeltes, not far off the road is a car park and you then walk to the site and arrive at an original inturned entrance (with a church just inside). This is a large castro with an internal area of about 4.5 hectares although there is nothing to see inside. The best thing to do is turn right at the entrance and walk around the outside of the walls (takes about 1 hour). There are signboards but they were in very poor condition in 2012.

The walls are immediately impressive, dry-stone construction standing 3m to 4m high and dating to the 2nd century BC, built by the *Vettones* tribe, with some 1st century AD Roman additions especially around the entrances. These are partially reconstructed (from around 2001) resulting from the excavation and clearance of fallen material around the outside of the walls, in places it is possible to see the difference between the original and reconstructed wall.

Other than the complete circuit of walls the interesting points to see are the areas of piedras hincadas and the engravings on some wall stones. The engravings, mainly of horses and deer plus one of a wolf with an open mouth bearing massive fangs, usually on the lower parts of the wall and around 10cm to 30cm long, are particularly rare and important but quite difficult to see so persevere. Some good engravings are visible to the left of a blocked entrance but the best are further around the circuit either side of a narrow (probably original) entrance with steps. To the right of this are further carvings on a horizontal slab at the base of the wall, several horses, one with a rider. From here you can go into the interior and cut across to the church and main entrance.

Having visited this site it is worth going to the small museum 1km away in Yecla de Yeltes (restricted access). The museum is situated in the Plaza Mayor

Figure 7.3. Castro de Yecla la Vieja

Figure 7.4. Horse engraving, Castro de Yecla la Vieja

(if it is closed try getting the key from the building to the left, the one with the clock). It contains a small but good display (in Spanish) including material from the excavations at the castro and general interpretations of the castro culture. The highlights are an impressive boar verraco and two carved Celtic heads, all supposedly from the castro.

Castro de El Castillo (Saldeana)

Unrestricted access

This site is not as easy to access as the two above and involves driving along a rough track and then walking. Once there it is overgrown and not well looked after although the walls are impressive as is the location.

Six kilometres north of the CL517 east of Lumbrales take the DSA573 to Saldeana. Continue through the town and take the paved track to the left. Where the paving ends and the track bifurcates take the unmade track straight on to the car parking area, then walk along the fairly rough path to the castro.

Occupying a granite promontory overlooking the Río Huebra, this castro has walls (partly restored) still standing six to eight metres high and two to four metres thick. There are two entrances and an impressive campo de piedras hincadas. Interpretation boards (in Spanish) explain the Iron Age origins and Roman re-use of the site.

Ávila and around

Ávila is famous for its medieval walls and Saint Teresa, and is a World Heritage Site situated about 100km west of Madrid. It is a highland area, the plain itself lying some 1,100m above sea level, and is watered by a small river, the Adajo, which is a tributary of the much larger Duero which runs into Portugal. The surrounding landscape includes the archaeological sites described below, and is good, gentle walking country.

The origins of Ávila are uncertain although it was a Roman town with no evidence of occupation earlier than about AD 50. Earlier activity in the area is suggested by the recent excavations of the town walls at the Roman entrance of San Vicente which produced a re-used verraco embedded into the wall. The main delights of the town are now its atmospheric narrow winding streets and rich architecture dating mainly to the 16th century together with one of the best-preserved medieval town walls anywhere in the world. Rising to a height of 12m the wall has 88 watch towers and eight monumental gates, much dating to the 11th century but with many additions of re-used Roman and Muslim stones.

Historically little is known about the area, even in the Roman period. Hannibal captured the town of Salamanca 100km to the west in 219 BC, but the Romans did not take over the area until around 50 BC. By the first century AD Ávila

(*Obila* or *Abila*) was one of the major towns of the local tribe, the *Vettones*, now Romanised. Archaeologically these have much in common with the better-known Celtiberians further to the north, with castros like those in Asturias (see Section 3 of this book) and the defended oppida of *Numantia*, captured by Scipio in 132 BC, (see below).

Ávila Provincial Museum

Plaza de Nalvillos, 3
Restricted access

The museum is in the Casa de los Deanes, a 16th century Renaissance palace. It houses a wide range of cultural materials from the area including rural enthnography, local history, art and archaeology. The displays are in Spanish only. Not surprisingly it has a very good display on the castros of the area and if you are going to visit any of those then you should start here.

The displays start with a chronological breakdown of the archaeology of the area. It includes explanatory models, for example of the Bernuy dolmen (see below). The highlights, however, have to be the castros as there is much excavated material on display from the sites described below and others. For example the tremendous swords and daggers from burials at El Raso; the grave goods from the excavations at La Mesa de Miranda and the fantastic collection of sheet bronze bowls from Castro de los Castillejos. There is a good explanation and display of verracos including some from Las Cogotas and the enigmatic Toros de Guisando (see below). More prehistory is covered upstairs, on the veranda and in the garden.

Figure 7.5. Verracos in Ávila Provincial Museum

Next door to the museum is the 13th century church of Santo Tomé El Viejo which is an annexe of the museum. This houses some interesting Roman material including animal figures, mosaics and funeral stelae, as well as monumental inscriptions, architectural and funeral elements dating from the Middle and Modern Ages. There is also a verraco.

Located in the Amblés Valley to the west of Ávila are three castros that are worth visiting with a lot of archaeology to see together with some walking through beautiful countryside. There are more castros and verracos than are described here and it is worth visiting the Tourist Information Office in Ávila (Avenida de Madrid, 39) for information on the 'Ruta de Castros y Verracos'.

Castro de Las Cogotas

Unrestricted access

Northwest of Ávila from the A50 take the AV804 minor road to the village of Cardeñosa. Once in the village it is worth visiting the Las Cogotas interpretation centre before proceeding to the site:

Aula Arqueológica

Calle de María Vela, 1
Restricted access

This is in the old town hall, next to the church (which is worth looking inside if it is open). Displays here on all aspects of the castro include good reconstructions and videos (in Spanish). The local rock is granite and a video shows how this can be split to produce the massive slabs used in the castro's ramparts. Piedras hincadas are explained and on the top floor is an excellent model of the whole castro together with interactive displays on many topics.

Leave the village on the AV804 back towards Ávila and on the left is a signposted track to the castro. This is about a 2k walk or you can drive closer to the site. If you can walk it is well worth doing across the attractive granite landscape, look out for signs of recent quarrying. The castro occupies a small natural elevation of the land, with two striking rounded granite ridges, to which it owes its name.

There have been two periods of excavation at Las Cogotas, the first started in the late 1920s within the castro and the necropolis where 1,469 graves were found. These excavations were important in establishing the late Bronze Age culture of the area followed by the Iron Age (still known as Cogotas I and II).

The second campaign was in the 1980s when a part of the site dedicated to pottery production was threatened by the construction of the reservoir which today covers much of that area. Other than the location and views the main things to see are the reconstructed main entrance and an area of housing.

Figure 7.6. An entrance at Castro de Las Cogotas

There are two fortified enclosures giving a maximum area of 14.5ha, with three entrances in each, one being reconstructed. This is an impressive stone wall and the levels below the slate line are original dating to 300 BC to 100 BC. Outside this entrance and around part of the walls is an impressive field of piedras hincadas which give a real feel for how difficult it would be to attack the walls through this mass of stones. In the interior of the site are platforms for rectangular buildings. There is a boar verraco found somewhere near the entrance now displayed in the Calvo Sotelo de Ávila square, Madrid.

Castro de La Mesa de Miranda

Unrestricted access

Take the AV110 24km west of Ávila to the small town of Chamartín de la Sierra. The Aula Arquaeologica (interpretation centre) is on the outskirts of town in the old town hall (Calle Canchas del Rio). It contains good explanations of the *Vettone* their castros and especially their burials with models and display boards (in Spanish). Look out for the bull verraco in the attractive square outside the current town hall.

On the other side of town take the Calle de Prado Viejo towards the cemetery, continue straight ahead where the track turns into a path. It is best to walk from here, about 3km, across nice rolling landscape with holm oaks, granite boulders and grazing black bulls. The site is fenced although access is at any time. The site dominates an extensive territory of good grazing lands highlighting the importance of cattle to the *Vettone* people.

Figure 7.7. Castro de La Mesa de Miranda

This is a large and complex site covering nearly 30ha so there is a lot to see. There are several interpretation boards (in Spanish) with good reconstruction drawings. The site has three large walled enclosures enclosed by massive stone ramparts with fields of piedras hincadas around parts of the outside, the earliest constructed in the 5th century BC with activity probably continuing until the 2nd century BC. Many lengths of walling are well preserved as are some of the entrances. There are also good examples of piedras hincadas outside the first and second enclosures.

There is also a large cemetery known as La Osera. The site was excavated between 1932 and 1945 mainly concentrating on the cemetery which lies about 350m outside the main gate of first enclosure. It was completely excavated producing 2,230 graves and more than 5,000 metal grave goods making this one of the largest and most extensively explored Iron Age cemeteries in the Iberian peninsula.

Figure 7.8. The cemetery at Castro de La Mesa de Miranda

Many burials were cremations within pots placed into holes in the ground with grave goods and then covered by a stone slab. Others were in groups protected by stone cairns, about 60 of them, between 2m and 6m in diameter oval and circular, some with standing stone stelae. Some of these are still visible today. The grave goods ranged from small personal ornaments to large daggers and swords and were either placed within the urns or next to them. It is not clear where the actual cremations took place as no evidence of pyres was found within the cemetery.

Castro de Ulaca

Unrestricted access

Situate south-west of Ávila, take the N502, after 24km turn left on the AVP410 through the villages of Solosancho and Villaviciosa (both places have verracos on display). A few hundred metres on the other side of Villaviciosa, along the Calle Ulaca, is the parking place for the castro with an information board. From there you walk to the site but being as the castro covers over 80ha, it's the largest of the *Vettone* castros, you need to be prepared for a long visit and a fairly tough walk. Having said that the site is very impressive and has some unique features that can't be seen anywhere else.

The castro is positioned on a raised promontory giving good views northwards across the fertile Amblés Valley. It has been a protected monument since 1931 and since 1994 has been a protected archaeological zone, the highest level of protection under Spanish law. No doubt the reason for this is the preservation of its unusual elements such as the sacrificial altar as well as its 3km long external wall dating mainly to the 3rd/2nd centuries BC although the castro probably started in the 5th century.

In the north-western sector of the site is the sacrificial altar carved from a massive block of granite. This enigmatic feature has a flight of steps leading up to a series of hollows/small pools in the rock, some natural and some carved, connected by channels. The accepted interpretation of this is that it was a place of ritual sacrifice (of what isn't known) with the blood and/or sacred libations running down the channels, being in a very visible place so that the congregation could watch the proceedings. Less than 200m away is the so-called sauna which is partly carved into the rock and partly consisting of built walls. Again, its interpretation is ritual, perhaps to do with warrior initiation, and has been likened to the saunas found in some of the north-western castros (see Section 3 of this book). The other unique feature is the watchtower which again may have some kind of public/ritual use.

Figure 7.9. The altar in Castro de Ulaca

This huge site has 3km of a massive stone-built ramparts around it, sections of which are well preserved some having been reconstructed. There are also several gateways. It is clear from the surface remains that the interior was divided into zones for different activities including the sacred/ritual zone and the domestic zone for houses. The stone foundations of the houses are well preserved in places numbering approximately 250 within the enclosure and another 50 outside the walls. It has been suggested that this represents a population of 1,000 or so people at the height of the castro's occupation. The houses are square or rectangular varying in size and complexity from 45 square metres with two rooms to 250 square metres with many more rooms. Door jambs are visible as large slabs of granite, and two houses excavated in the 1970s showed fireplaces, benches and storage areas. It is not known what the rest of the walls were made from nor the rooves although these were probably thatch. Some of the houses have evidence for a porch and all have their entrance facing sunrise to the east.

The final thing to notice as you walk around this wonderful site are the contemporary granite quarries. These are located in the western area of the enclosure where they seem to be for house construction due to the smaller size of the blocks being prepared whereas in the south-western areas the larger blocks are for the rampart walls. It is possible to see how they broke off blocks of granite by hammering wedges into the natural fractures in the bedrock. The initial rough blocks were then finished before being moved to their final destination. Rough, partially finished and finished blocks can be seen lying around the quarry areas as if the work was suddenly abandoned. The obvious skill involved in this process does raise the possibility of their being specialist quarry workers.

Castro El Raso de Candeleda

Unrestricted access

This site is further away from Ávila but worth a visit for its dramatic location in the foothills of the Sierra de Gredos and also because there are good reconstructions of *Vettone* houses. Take the N502 south and after about 50km turn right to Arenas de San Pedro on the AV923 and continue through to the town of Candeleda. Go through Candeleda and turn right to El Raso. Go through the village and take the Calle Jesús Jiménez Busto following the signs to the castro.

Before leaving El Raso there is a small museum to visit (access restricted) in the centre of the village giving a good background to the castro, the *Vettone* ways of life and burial. You can also book guided tours of the castro here.

El Raso, discovered in 1931, covers about 20ha with a surrounding stone rampart of nearly 2km in length with towers and bastions in places and a ditch at the front. Parts of the defences are visible although the main attraction here are

Figure 7.10. Houses in Castro El Raso de Candeleda

the houses. Originally there would have been around 300 rectangular houses of different sizes packed close together in a 'domestic zone' suggesting a population of around 2,500 people. Excavations since the 1970s have revealed a large area of houses as well as exploring the necropolis. Two houses have been reconstructed and act as an interpretation centre offering a good explanation of the *Vettone* in this area.

It seems that the people of this area initially lived in a small settlement called El Castañar near the modern village before constructing the defended site of El Raso. Excavations of the cemetery there produced many artefacts including Greek wine cups showing links with the Mediterranean cultures further south. This occupation dates 5th to 3rd centuries BC with El Raso dating to the 2nd and 1st centuries BC. When the Romans took control of the area all defended sites were dismantled by order and people moved to the lower valleys.

Verracos de los Toros de Guisando

Unrestricted access

Southeast of Ávila on the N403, south on the AV904 just before San Martín de Valdeiglesias.

This set of four verracos are without doubt the most famous in the Iberian peninsula and if you like these enigmatic sculptures you are in for a treat. Exactly when they were placed in their current position is unknown but an important treaty bearing their name and unifying Castile was signed there in 1468. In the early 17th century Cervantes refers to them several times in Don Quiote and Lorca draws on their symbolic power in one of his poems.

Figure 7.11. Verracos de los Toros de Guisando

The four granite bulls are imposing, standing 1.5m high and 2.8m long, originally on bases which are now mostly covered. They are aligned with their heads to the west and some details are well preserved. Across the four indications of jaws and ears can be seen together with holes for the fixing of horns, there are also wrinkles in the skin on the neck, forelegs, knees, back and tail. On the sides of some of them are zigzag patterns. Three of the sculptures show Latin inscriptions on their side indicating that they were perhaps re-used as funerary monuments in the Roman period. Only one inscription can be read today on the right flank of the bull at the northern end. It is dated to the first century AD and informs us that the inscription was ordered by a certain Longinus in memory of his father Prisco, of the Calaeticos: LONGINUS PRISCO CALAETIQ (um) PATRI F (aciendum) C (uravit).

It is generally thought that the bulls would have originally stood individually in the meadows and grazing areas in the surrounding landscape. Excavation around the bulls in 1946 failed to find anything which at least confirms that they are not an *in situ* element of a burial monument.

If you want a change from castros, less than 10km east of Ávila there is an interesting dolmen:

Dolmen Prado de las Cruces, Bernuy

Unrestricted access

Dolmen that are well preserved and accessible are relatively rare in this area compared to other regions of Spain. This one is easily reachable by taking the AV-500 local road from Ávila to the small village of Bernuy-Salinero. The site is signposted at the entrance to the village and can be accessed by a path on the left of the road. You leave your car after 200m and then walk the remaining 400m, the dolmen is on the left surrounded by a low stone wall.

Figure 7.12. Dolmen Prado de las Cruces, Bernuy

This is a passage grave represented by upright stones, orthostats, still in position in the ground with those of the chamber being bigger than those of the passage. The passage into the burial chamber is 5m long and oriented to the east, a direction which is common with this type of tomb and thought to be related to the direction of sunrise. The burial chamber is oval, 3.5m by 4m. The whole structure was originally covered by a cairn of stones roughly 22m in diameter which has now mainly gone although remnants can be seen. Limited excavation has suggested that the tomb was constructed at the end of the 4th millennium BC and remodelled later to become a Bronze Age round barrow in approximately 1,500 BC. On the ground there is no evidence of this second phase.

If you are travelling north from Ávila towards Valladolid and want to see some interesting rock art it is worth stopping at:

Arte Rupestre de Domingo García

Unrestricted access

About 56km north of Ávila, N403, N601 turn right on the CL605 to Santa María la Real de Nieva then the SG3411 towards Migueláñez. The site is signposted 'Grabados rupestres' on the left, drive up the track to the stone hut beneath the ruined church on the hill, the Ermita de San Isidro, which is worth visiting and has rock-cut graves. This is a lovely peaceful place with good views.

There are several panels of rock art with explanatory boards (in Spanish) here and you need to explore the area. There seems to be a range of dates for the art from possible Palaeolithic images, some Bronze/Iron Age, medieval plus modern graffiti, although the site is of importance for its Palaeolithic art, for example the horse on Panel 4 and the deer on Panel 1. The art is engraved onto bedrock and is difficult to see in places.

Panel 4 shows a dense covering of possible Bronze/Iron Age figures with a range of weapons, some horses and riders. Between panels 4 and 2 are good small panels (but no associated explanatory board) of possible Iron Age horsemen with weapons. Panel 7 is furthest past the church, 500m or so along a rough path.

While in the area just north of Segovia it is worth going about 50km east of Domingo García to see the tremendous caves at:

Cueva de Los Enebralejos

Restricted access

Signposted from the N110 about 10km before the junction with the A1 on the outskirts of Prádena.

This is a massive complex of caves with very impressive formations of stalactites and stalagmites. There is also archaeology in the form of Palaeolithic and early Bronze Age engravings and painted figures as well as evidence for occupation and burial. The small site museum has background information and interesting reconstructions of a Bronze Age house and artefacts.

Burgos and around

The delights of the old quarter of Burgos are crowned by the magnificent Gothic cathedral, often cited as the finest in Spain. Started in the 13th century and completed in the 15th, it is a huge and intricate complex of architectural delights and don't miss the tomb of the legendary El Cid in the interior. Burgos also boasts two museums which are essential for prehistorians.

The Museum of Burgos

Calle Miranda, 13
Restricted access

Housed in a beautiful Renaissance palace, the Casa de Miranda, this museum explains the cultural and historical development of the region from Palaeolithic times to the modern period. The building next door, the Casa de Íñigo Angulo, is the fine arts collection.

The archaeological displays are chronological starting with Palaeolithic material from the Ojo Guareña caves and the internationally important site of Atapuerca (below). The displays are good and informative, our highlights include the display of dolmen and of the Iron Age cemeteries, especially the Necrópolis de La Polera, Ubierna with incredible bronzes including brooches and belt buckles within stone circular graves with burial stelae. The section on castros includes a reconstruction of the walls at Trasmonte, very well done.

The Museum of Human Evolution

Restricted access

Situated on the south bank of the River Arlanzón close to the town centre, this ultra-modern building is a museum as well as a research and conference centre. It was established primarily to display and explain the internationally important finds from the site of Atapuerca which is 17km to the east (see below). It provides everything you ever wanted to know about human evolution, and a lot more, through innovative displays and interactive exhibits, in both Spanish and English. More than 200 original human remains are displayed including Homo Antecessor, the oldest from anywhere in Europe. A visit here is highly recommended before going to Atapuerca where you can see where many of the remains were found.

The museum opens with an explanation of the Karst, limestone, geology around Atapuerca producing caves which were so attractive to early humans. There is also a section on the history of archaeological exploration and finds. The displays then proceed chronologically and here we mention some of our favourites. The finds from the Sima de los Huesos are remarkable for being the oldest and largest human fossil bearing deposit in the world. In this cave the remains of at least 28 individuals were found, claimed to be the first mass grave in history, both sexes and a range of ages up to 50 years old but mostly teenagers and young adults. These are Homo Heidelbergensis, ancestors of the Neanderthals, dating to at least 350,000 years ago. Found with the bones was a handaxe,

Figure 7.13. The Museum of Human Evolution, Burgos (Photo: Simon and Barbara Maddison)

Figure 7.14. Homo habilis, The Museum of Human Evolution, Burgos (Photo: Simon and Barbara Maddison)

known as 'Excalibur', important for being possibly the oldest example of an artefact being buried with a human thus suggesting that 'symbolic thought and imagination' was in existence at a much earlier date than previously suggested. The pathology of some of these skeletons suggests that the older members were 'looked after', with evidence for hip problems, tooth abscesses, deafness and one with a deformed skull.

The Cueva Mayor is interesting in demonstrating deep stratigraphy illustrating occupation levels from 6,200 years ago through the Neolithic, Chalcolithic, Bronze Age, Iron Age, Roman and medieval periods. Another exhibit explains the process of excavation and the various techniques used in post excavation analysis and interpretation. The theory of evolution is explained concentrating on the body and the brain, senses and speaking showing how 'being human' is so complicated. An excellent and fun exhibit is the large wire 'brain' that when inside shows neural activity.

The life size models of human development from the early Australopithecus to Homo Sapiens are accompanied by very detailed accounts of each. Finally, the evolution of cultural aspects covers things like flint knapping and tool making, 'fire through the ages', the development of art and symbolism including the earliest burials. Don't miss the cinema in the round.

Atapuerca archaeological site

Restricted access

Signposted from Ibeas de Juarros on the N120 8km east of Burgos, take the BUV7012 to the left.

This limestone ridge is rich in evidence for early humans with over 300 'sites' known, it is now possible to see in detail three of them which have some of the oldest human activity in Europe going back 1.2 million years. The earliest archaeological discoveries were due to a British company mining iron ore in the 19th century blasting a railway cutting through the rock. The irony is that the mining only lasted for 10 years before being abandoned leaving some of the most important evidence for early humans known anywhere. The visit today takes you through this cutting where three areas of activity are exposed and explained in detail. There is still limited excavation which takes place in the summer.

The first site is the Sima del Elefante. Excavations her over decades have revealed an exceptional section through more than 20 metres of stratigraphy showing successive occupation of the cave. The earliest layers date to 1.2 million years ago and represent the earliest humans in this area and a warm climate. The latest layers date to 200,000 years ago and contain cold species such as mammoth and reindeer together with flint tools.

Figure 7.15. Atapuerca archaeological site (© Instituto del Patrimonio Cultural de España. Ministerio de Educación, Cultura y Deporte)

The next two sites are close together, the Galería and the Gran Dolina. Again, the stratigraphy shows multiple occupation levels. One is the campsite of 'the boy', a skeleton dating to 800,000 years ago, probably about 16 years old when he died, 1.65m tall. There is some evidence suggesting cannibalism. Nearby is activity showing that a later group of Homo Heidelbergensis lived here, similar to the Sima de los Huesos, which is only 2km away (see above). Here a 15m deep hole in the rock was used to capture animals where they were butchered and then taken to the nearby campsite for consumption.

Overall the evidence at Atapuerca is remarkable both for the time depth represented and the richness of finds. Together with a visit to the Museum of Human Evolution in Burgos it provides one of the best early human experiences in Europe.

Soria and around

Moving to the eastern fringes of Castilla y León we leave the territory of the pre-Roman *Vettones* and enter that of the Celtiberians who occupied the eastern and northern meseta. The main archaeological site to visit at Soria is the important Celtiberian and Roman town of Numancia (Numantia). It took the Roman army approximately 150 years to conquer the Iberian peninsula, a long and hard campaign which was most difficult for them in the northern regions. The Celtiberian wars were a critical phase of the occupation with Numancia holding out for twenty years finally to fall to an eleven-month siege, 153 BC to 133 BC, according to Classical accounts. It was not until 50 BC that lasting peace was established.

Before moving on to describe Numancia it is worth mentioning the site of Tiermes that lies some 25km to the south-west of Soria. This was another important Celtiberian town that put up strong resistance to the Romans then to be developed into a major Roman town. It has been extensively excavated and there is much to see there including unusual rock-cut Celtiberian houses amongst the extensive Roman remains many cut into the sandstone rock. There is also a small museum close to the site.

Oppida de Numancia

Restricted access

North of Soria on the N111, Numancia is signposted from the centre of Garray. In this village is an Archaeology Teaching Centre where there are good models, projections and reconstructions explaining the site and its history.

At the entrance to Numancia there are videos and signs (in Spanish) together with leaflets all of which provide a lot of information on the site. The importance of Numancia in a nationalistic sense is marked by an obelisk commemorating the fight against the Romans and every July there is a re-enacted battle within the ruins.

This is a big site with a lot to see and it's best to follow the marked route which has display boards. On your way around look out for four white monoliths in the landscape spaced around the town, these mark the positions of Roman siege camps. The visible remains at Numancia are mainly from the period of Roman occupation and the subsequent 'Romanised' town, the original Celtiberian structures are hard to find. The areas of excavation, mainly from the late 19th century, cover various types of buildings and street layouts. There are reconstructed houses, a Celtiberian one with a loom, quern and tools and a Roman one with pots and other daily artefacts.

Figure 7.16. A reconstructed Celtiberian house in Oppida de Numancia

To enhance the visit it is worth going to the:

Museo Numantino, Soria

Paseo el Espolón, Soria
Restricted access

This museum has three floors and material from the Palaeolithic period to Roman and is particularly good for artefacts and explanations regarding Numancia. The displays are mainly in Spanish with some English in the Celtiberian section.

It has a display on the barrows of the Ambrona Valley, especially La Sima and La Peña de la Abuela (see below). The second floor is dedicated to Numancia and its inhabitants with a lot of metalwork and pottery on display, some of it superb such as the case of decorated bronze belt buckles. There is a reconstructed house with furniture. The explanation of the name 'Celtiberian', how it originated and the history of those peoples is very good. Also how for political reasons the Romans chose specific Celtiberian towns to develop from 50 BC onwards, Numancia and Tiermes being two of them.

While in Soria if you are interested in rock art then visit:

The Valonsadero Valley, arte rupestre

Open access

Approximately 10km to the west of Soria on the N234 turn right to the Valonsadero. This is a large natural park area with lots of activities especially good for walking. Look for signs to 'Pinturas rupestres'. Proceed past the restaurant on the left, stop at the next car park on the left and the path leads to rocks below the car park. Here are a series of 11 panels of art with fences and explanatory boards.

The art dates to the 3rd/2nd millennia BC, the Chalcolithic and early Bronze Ages and comprises mainly red ochre paintings many in shallow rock shelters. Humans and animals are depicted along with a whole range of different geometric patterns, Panel 4 is very good. Panel 5 is further along the path up the valley, turn right at the small concrete signpost. Panel 7 is very mysterious with jellyfish-like motifs. Panels 9, 10 and 11 are a ten-minute walk from 8, 10 is especially worth seeing with very distinctive human figures.

Figure 7.17. Display of an excavation, Museum of Ambrona

Ambrona and around

This area is approximately 70km south of Soria, centred on the small town of Ambrona just west of the junction of the A15 and A2.

Museum of Ambrona

Avenida del Museo
Restricted access

Between Torralba and Ambrona, take the NA4099, follow the railway line, signposted right at the convent. Look out for the giant mammoth!

This is an open-air Palaeolithic 'kill' site with evidence for various fauna including mammoths, rhinos and panthers all dating to approximately 400,000 to 200,000 years ago. There is a small museum with some good displays based on old and more recent excavations. The points of controversy are whether this was a place where Palaeolithic hunters actually killed animals or whether the animals were already dead and the hunters just butchered them there. There also is some discussion as to whether the flint tools found there are contemporary with the animal bones.

The Ambrona Valley

Unrestricted access

This is a very attractive valley with good walking. Three rivers meet here and it is surrounded by highlands, within a relatively small area there are over 100 prehistoric burial mounds. The attraction was probably the number of lakes and lagoons which attracted animals and, therefore, hunting humans, it is still wet. While walking along the valley it is possible to pick out the remains of burial mounds although the main attractions are the two that have been excavated and presented, La Peña de la Abuela and Túmulo de La Sima.

Figure 7.18.
Túmulo de La Sima

Just outside the town, car park on the left, is a reconstruction of La Peña de la Abuela, this is not its original position. Here you can see a reconstructed section through the barrow, the beehive structure and a layer of lime (giving rise to the name 'lime-kiln tombs) indicating that human remains were burnt here *in situ*.

A track to the left after about 500m on the road to Conquezuela, is the path along the valley leading to La Sima through a wet area with a seasonal lake on the left, the site is in the mid distance on the right in a field before a ridge. The barrow has been completely excavated and partially reconstructed.

There are three phases to the construction of this mound: firstly the 'lime kiln' phase with the burning of bones; secondly a tholos tomb built over the top of the lime layer and finally the Bell Beaker burials. Most of what you see are the remains of the Phase 2 tomb with a circular dry-stone walled chamber which would have originally closed to a corbelled roof. The orthostats of the passage leading into the chamber still survive. The tomb would have been partially covered by a cairn of stones. There is a stone box within the chamber which contained human bones. Radiocarbon dating of this phase is 1,600 BC and of the first phase from charcoal 1,800 BC to 2,000 BC. There is some remodelling of the structure in Beaker times and the burial of two adults with a range of Beaker pottery a copper flat axe and daggers, flint arrowheads and stone wrist guards – the typical package of Beaker grave goods found across Europe.

In the nearby small village of Miño de Medinaceli (not the larger nearby Medinaceli) there is a small interpretation centre for the two excavated barrows with general background information. This is in the old schoolhouse although it is a recent building (the opening hours seem to be very restricted but we managed to get the key from the bar next door). There is a good model of the three phases of La Sima with an explanation of the excavations, also a model human with artefacts.

Figure 7.19. Beaker period artefacts from the Túmulo de La Sima (© Interpretation Centre, Miño de Medinaceli

Abrigo de Carlos Álvarez

Unrestricted access

On the road from Miño to Conquezuela, the GU136, is some interesting early Bronze Age (*c.* 2,000 BC) rock art easily accessible with a display board. Stop at the small church built into the cliff on the right, the Ermita de Santa Cruz. Where the cliff ends to the left is a signboard, there is a low cave or more accurately rock shelter behind. The panel of red ochre paintings are at head height at the back of the rock shelter. There are two human figures at the top, a possible boat and a circular sun-like motif. Over on the left of these are cup marks and an artificial 'basin' cut into the rock floor, of unknown date.

Extremadura

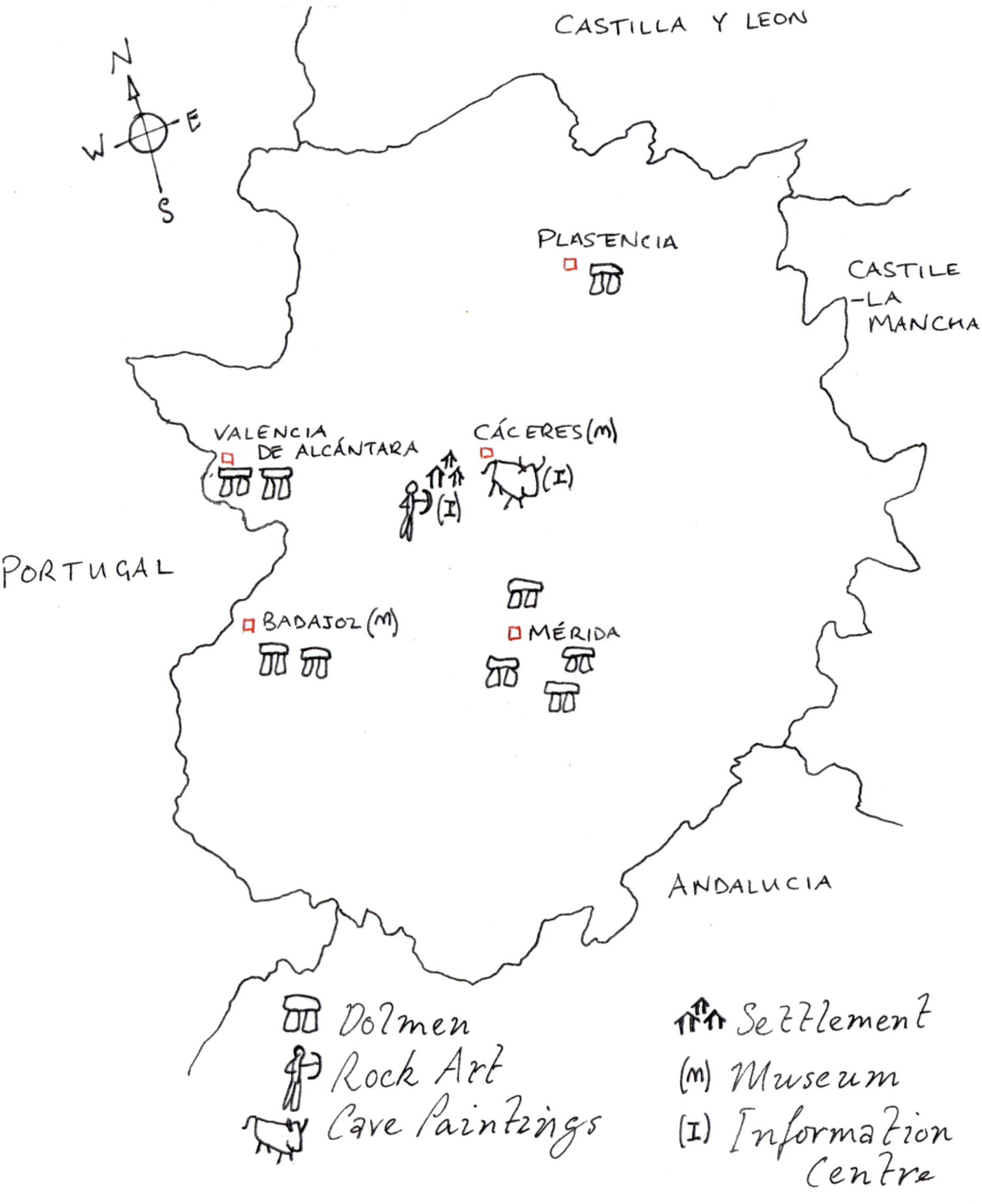

Chapter 8
Extremadura

In many ways the region of Extremadura is a hidden gem of Spain with sweeping landscapes, cities with fascinating histories and charming small villages. Other than in the large cites of Cáceres, Badajoz and Mérida you will encounter very few tourists in this sparsely populated area bordering Portugal. Beware of the climate here though as in the summer months it is extremely hot while in the winter very cold.

Although bordered in the north, east and south by wooded sierras, the central and southern areas of Extremadura that we are describing here are a distinctive type of pastureland called *dehesas*. The extensive grasslands that stretch for hundreds of kilometres, parched yellow in the summer, are covered with evergreen Holm and cork oak trees. In the autumn pigs eat the Holm acorns, a diet that produces the best *jamón* in Spain while many cork oaks show stripped bark used for a variety of products not least to cork wine bottles. The black fighting bulls are also bred in this area and can be seen grazing between the trees.

Travelling south through Extremadura towards Cáceres if you have time it is worth trying to find an incredible dolmen which has been called the 'Stonehenge of Spain' in the media.

Dolmen de Guadalperal

Unrestricted access

It is situated about 65km east of Plasencia along the A5 towards Madrid, at Bermejo turn right on the minor road CC33 to the villages of El Gordo and Berrocalejo.

The dolmen was first discovered in 1926 and excavated by the German archaeologist Hugo Obermaier before being submerged beneath the waters of a reservoir in 1963, the Embalse de Valdecañas. Due to years of draught and falling water levels, the dolmen was rediscovered on a NASA satellite image in 2019 (hence the Stonehenge media hype) and is now visible for much of the time on the edge of the reservoir.

Unfortunately, it is almost impossible to walk along the edge of the reservoir to the site and the only way to get to it is by boat. We did it by contacting a company called Valdecañas Multiventura based in Berrocalejo who have a social media presence but no offices or website. At the time of writing (June 2022) the contact was Ruben who is contactable through the Bar El Arenal.

Figure 8.1. Dolmen de Guadalperal

Approaching the dolmen by boat shows how impressive it is and gives a good idea of how big the original cairn must have been that covered the passage and chamber. It consists of approximately 150 granite orthostats of different sizes in concentric rings forming an oval chamber 5m at its widest point. Leading into the chamber from the reservoir side is an access corridor about 21m long and 1.4m wide also formed of orthostats. At the end of the corridor, at the entrance to the chamber is a free-standing menhir which has a snake (or perhaps a representation of the Tagus River which originally flowed close to the dolmen) and several cup marks carved on it. Unfortunately, these are very difficult to see as all the stones are covered with a white encrustation due to being in the water for so long although drawings done during the excavation do exist.

The evidence uncovered by Obermaier including axes, flint knives, a copper punch and pottery, date the tomb to the late Neolithic/Chalcolithic, *c.* 2,000 BC, as would be expected for this type of burial monument. He also excavated a settlement nearby with houses and artefacts which suggested to him that the tomb builders lived there.

The covering cairn of small stones was circular and the remains are clear to see. This form of dolmen, with a circular chamber and entrance passage is common in this area and across the border into Portugal where they are called Anta-type dolmen. They are also sometimes referred to as Tholoi tombs, Greek for dome and referencing ancient Greek tombs with circular corbelled rooves.

Central Extremadura: around Cáceres

This visit has to start with seeing Cáceres itself and the archaeological museum which contains material and information about the megalithic tombs (dolmen) around Valencia de Alcantára described below and much more. The ancient walled old town, Ciudad Monumental, dates mostly to the 15th and 16th centuries but replaces many older buildings. It is one of the most important collections of extant medieval buildings in Spain and the whole is a World Heritage Site. Also visit at night if you possibly can as many of the most impressive buildings are lit creating an almost fantasy scene. A few hours wandering around the cobbled streets, taking in the many grand family palaces, churches, the cathedral and the town walls with splendid gates is well worth it.

Within the old town, easy to find using the map from the Tourist Information Office, is Cáceres Museum housed in the beautiful 16th century Casa de las Veletas, a family palace. This building became the museum in the 1930s based on archaeological collections of local antiquarians and scholars first brought together in the late 19th century. Look out for the gargoyles and the enamelled ceramic waterspouts which adorn the front of the building.

Cáceres Museum

Plaza de las Veletas
Restricted access

There is an English leaflet available at reception, limited English information within the displays.

Rooms 1 to 3 cover the prehistoric periods, the first having material from the Palaeolithic and Neolithic including pottery, beads and flints from the Valencia de Alcantára tombs described below.

Room 2 is devoted to the Copper and Bronze Ages and has an excellent collection including late Bronze Age (9th to 7th centuries BC) carved warrior gravestones, stelae, (as in Figure 8.9). These include images of swords, shields and what appear to be four-wheeled wagons drawn by horses. One has been re-used in the Roman period with a super-imposed Latin inscription dedicated to 'Alluquius, son of Protaedus', both local names. To illustrate that stone carving may be a long tradition there are also early Bronze Age, *c.* 2,000 BC, carved figures and faces on stones. There is also a collection of very unusual bronzes including pieces of a bed dating to 7th/6th centuries BC with representations of animal and human heads, also sheet bronze bowls and containers and spectacular gold bracelets and a torc (neck-ring) dating to the 10th to 8th centuries BC.

Figure 8.2. Cáceres Museum, Room 2

Room 3 covers the Iron Age and has a good collection of pottery, iron daggers and a host of other material culture. There is also a small stone verraco, a carved boar with a face and an inscribed stone with at least two words in the Tartessian script important for showing possible links with further south.

Going through Rooms 4 and 5, Roman, brings you to the inner courtyard of the palace with its eight Tuscan columns, and the stairs up to the ethnographic collection. This is interesting and contains information and material relating to various agricultural practices, many of which will have been unchanged since prehistoric times. Using ards for ploughing for example, and transhumance which is the annual moving of animals to upland pastures in the summer, and cheese and oil production.

It is also worth going down to the basement which is an Islamic water cistern, the only remaining part of what may have been the original castle. Also across the garden to the Fine Arts section housed in the original stables where the collection contains Miro paintings and Picasso drawings. Look out for two more verracos in the garden.

Cueva de Maltravieso and Interpretation Centre

Avenida de Cervantes
Cáceres
Restricted access

From the modern centre of Cáceres head for the southeastern suburbs along Avenida de Antonio Hurtado which changes into the Avenida de Cervantes, the centre is signposted along this road.

This is the best example of evidence for Palaeolithic occupation in Extremadura consisting of material culture and cave paintings. The entrance to the cave was discovered during mining in 1951 and five years later the local archaeologist Carlos Callejo discovered the paintings inside along with pottery, tools and bones of the Copper Age and Neolithic. Knowledge of the cave and its long

Figure 8.3. Art within the Cueva de Maltravieso

occupation has been greatly enhanced by excavation and research since 2001. The cave is closed to the public because of the sensitivity of the paintings, but the interpretation centre, which is at the mouth of the cave, offers an excellent account of the archaeology (in Spanish) including a reconstruction of the gallery with the paintings.

The centre contains displays of material from the excavations including flint tools, a bronze spearhead and a trepanned skull covering the Palaeolithic to Bronze Age periods, starting much earlier than the paintings. The art is thought to date from the Gravettian period (25,000 to 21,000 BC) and was found in a long narrow passage within the cave consisting of lines of black dots, lines, an engraved horse but mainly a series of about 60 human handprints in 20 panels. These are negatives outlined by red ochre and, interestingly, several have a little finger missing suggesting that they are perhaps of the same person. There is also a 3D video of the cave's interior which is fun to 'drive' and a film room showing life in the Palaeolithic.

If you are now heading to Valencia de Alcantára to see the megalithic tombs (described below) you will probably take the N521 direct route from Cáceres, in which case visit:

Los Barruecos, National Monument and Interpretation Centre

Malpartida de Cáceres
Restricted access

Take the N521 from Cáceres, about 10k go through Malpartida de Cáceres, Los Barruecos is signposted, take the Lavadero de Lanas and Museo Vostell road, follow the signs to the Interpretation Centre.

Figure 8.4. Los Barruecos

This is a fascinating area of lakes, low vegetation and huge eroded rounded granite boulders that rewards a few hours walking with fauna, flora and archaeology. These are all displayed and explained in the Interpretation Centre where a map and leaflet in English can be obtained. If you are lucky (and we weren't!) you can see a range of birds including Black Kites, Booted Eagles, Lesser Kestrels and colonies of White Storks.

The map shows various walks around the park ranging from 30 minutes to 4 hours together with the location of various archaeological remains including Roman rock-cut graves, a Roman villa, a Neolithic/Copper Age settlement and rock paintings. From the second car park the well signed path La Ruta de los Sentidos (wheel chair access, signed blue but not shown on the map – confusing!), is a beautiful walk through this dramatic landscape. At points along the route there are signposts to rock art on the boulders although these are extremely difficult to see, for example the engravings at Peña de la Horca, there are also information boards which are very useful. The next stop has some red figures, fenced off, which are just about discernible although it is difficult to differentiate between the human and animal figures as shown on the board. The path gets very confusing towards its end although if you follow the edge of the lake you return to the car park.

In terms of seeing archaeology this is a frustrating place to visit but wonderful to experience the unusual landscape with the chance of seeing some tremendous fauna.

Dolmen de Valencia de Alcantára

All unrestricted access

In the countryside around this small town is an important collection of Copper Age/Neolithic dolmen, numbering more than a hundred in total although no way near that many are accessible. Below we detail the easiest to reach. To obtain a map which shows the locations of some of the tombs go to the Tourist Information Office in Plaza Gregorio Bravo, Valencia de Alcantára. According to the information available there, there are (in theory) five Dolmen routes (Rutas de los Dólmenes). Despite spending several frustrating days following signs that led nowhere we failed to find Routes 1, 3 and 4. However, Routes 5 (five sites) and 2 (four sites) are fantastic and provide tremendous archaeology and beautiful walks (both of about two hours) through peaceful and interesting landscapes.

Route 5

Take the N521 out of Valencia in the direction of Portugal, after approximately 2km turn left towards Alcorneo. At the small village of Aceña de la Borrega find the church where there is a display board showing Route 5. Turn down the track

Figure 8.5. Dolmen Data 1

at the side of the church and after a hundred metres or so park at the sign, take the walking path to the left. This is a lovely walk along the tranquil valley with cork trees, granite boulders and small-scale agriculture. Follow the signs, turn right uphill, then left to the first two tombs:

Data 1 and 2

The nearest tomb shows some small kerbstones suggesting a cairn around the passage, there are seven uprights and a displaced capstone A couple of hundred metres away is the second tomb which shows much more of the cairn with a good passage and chamber uprights and displaced capstones. All the uprights are thin worked slabs. Both passages are oriented to the east as is often the case with these tombs. The location is important with good views both out from and of the tombs.

Retrace your steps to the main path and follow the signs to:

Dolmen del Mellizo

There is an interpretation board at the entrance, with some English, which is useful. This tomb is on a raised knoll which makes it visible from a distance away. It was excavated in 1985 and the finds, including pottery and flint tools, are in Cáceres museum. It has been reconstructed and is very well preserved giving a good impression of what the other less well preserved tombs must have looked like. The chamber is about 3m x 3.6m with capstones in place and the entrance passage again to the east. Notice the unusual stone between the passage and the chamber which may have been a blocking stone which closed the tomb when it was no longer used.

Figure 8.6. Dolmen del Mellizo

Continue along the path following the signs to the left to:

Dolmen de Cajirón 1

This tomb is damaged although it was excavated and restored somewhat in the 1990s, the finds of pottery, an unusual decorated 'plate' and a grinding stone are in Cáceres museum, there is an information board. The seven upright orthostats are impressive, the passage is visible as is a displaced capstone. Again, the position is important with good views making the tomb very visible from a distance.

Continue further along the path, following the signs to:

Dolmen de Cajirón 2

There is a notice board describing the excavations in the 1990s and the finds including decorated pot sherds, also in Cáceres museum. It also claims that a quarry for the stone used has been located about 50m to the southwest which is unusual. The tomb has been restored to show a good passage, seven uprights of the chamber measuring 2.7m by 3m and a capstone although there isn't much evidence of the cairn.

Return to the main path and then to the beginning of the trail, this is a circular route.

For all five of these tombs we have mentioned the probable importance of their location which were carefully chosen to be visible from a distance. Another aspect of this is that it was very clear to us that from all these sites a large and very prominent circular isolated boulder on the skyline is visible. Of course we will never know, but it is possible that natural features, and especially unusual natural features such as this boulder, may have held some sacred significance for these people and to be buried within sight of it was auspicious.

Route 2

Take the N521 out of Valencia in the opposite direction to Route 5. On the outskirts of town is a track on the right, just after the Polígono Industrial sign and before the major right-hand turn. There is a large display board with a map of Route 2. Continue down this track, park somewhere along it, after several hundred metres is a partially cobbled path to the left with side walls, take this.

Follow this path, it gets narrow and overgrown in places but stick with it, follow the occasional Dolmen signs, the first site is eventually on the right-hand side:

Dolmen de Zafra 1

This site is badly mutilated with only two uprights visible and a possible displaced capstone. It is positioned to look down a small valley.

Continue along the path following the signs to:

Dolmen de Zafra 2

This is the largest tomb in the area and is very impressive, there is a good interpretation board with some English. It was excavated in the 1960s and 1990s and has been restored, the finds are in Cáceres museum. These include pottery, a good collection of flint arrowheads, plaques decorated with triangles and zigzags and some beads, one of which is jet which is very rare and shows possible links with Northern Iberia where jet is found.

Figure 8.7. Dolmen de Zafra 2

Figure 8.8. Dolmen de Zafra 3

The chamber is 3.7m by 3m with large orthostats, one measuring 2.5m in height. There is a long passage, about 5m, facing east and several displaced capstones. One of the broken orthostats lying in the chamber has a curious vertical groove carved in it and holes which could be an attempt to fix it upright during the restoration rather than being original. There are many large stones around which may be cairn material. Again, the tomb is in a very prominent position with good views in several directions. Some of the natural granite boulders around the tomb have very curious 'basins' and 'steps' in them that don't look natural.

Return to the path and follow the signs to sites 3 and 4:

Dolmen de Zafra 3

One of the smallest tombs in the area, with a display board, excavated the same time as Zafra 2 but no artefacts were found, possibly due to the site being robbed. The site is very well preserved (and appears on postcards!) with seven uprights creating a chamber 2.6m x 2.2m and about 1.8m high with a single capstone. There is some evidence of the cairn. Located on a local high spot with views.

Continue on the path, turn left where signposted to:

Dolmen de Zafra 4

Again, there is an interpretation board suggesting that this tomb was also robbed of any artefacts that were originally within it. The tomb is poorly preserved and partly built into an old estate wall but has been reconstructed. There are five large orthostats but no evidence of the passage.

This is not a circular route so you have to retrace your steps back to the start.

Southern Extremadura, around Badajoz and Mérida

While in the area a visit to Mérida is a must to see some of the best-preserved Roman remains in Spain for which it is a UNESCO World Heritage site. With a population of more than 40,000 inhabitants it was the largest Roman city on the Iberian Peninsula and the theatre, amphitheatre, temples and other buildings are wonderfully preserved and presented.

Not far to the west of Mérida is the city of Badajoz which has an archaeological museum with a small but very interesting prehistoric collection including artefacts from and information on some of the dolmen described below.

Badajoz Provincial Archaeological Museum

Plaza José Álvarez y Sáenz de Buruaga
Restricted access

The museum is housed in a beautifully restored Renaissance palace within the Moorish fort area, the Alcazaba, situated on a hilltop north of the centre of town. There is a free audio guide in English although all the exhibit information is in Spanish only. The prehistoric collections on the first floor are relatively small but do contain some important objects, many appertaining to dolmen.

The material is laid out chronologically with the Neolithic/Chalcolithic containing some very good examples of decorated stone axes and decorated stone pendants which are unusual. There are also a range of beautifully crafted flint arrowheads found in the dolmen of Lacara (see below). There are also good examples of Bronze Age objects including axes, blades and chisels with an explanation of different casting techniques. Carved stone and bone pieces show wonderful anthropomorphic decoration, one with a strange 'collar and hat'.

The protohistoric room covers the period from the 8th century BC in the Mediterranean coastal areas subjected to contact with wider cultures from across that sea. These wider influences are shown by the sophistication of the bronze, iron and gold objects and by the range of thrown pots. There is a good explanation of the early writing of the Tartessians, *c.* 7th century BC, moving them out of the prehistoric world.

Not to be missed is the large and important collection of Late Bronze Age warrior burial stelae (gravestones), 8th to 7th centuries BC, displayed around the first-floor balcony. These show a wide range of carved decoration including a variety of symbols, human figures and even a chariot/wagon.

Dolmen del Prado de Lácara

Unrestricted access

About 16k north of Mérida, this dolmen is one of the largest and best preserved in Extremadura. From the A66 turn towards La Nava de Santiago on the EX214. The dolmen is signposted on the left into a small car park from where you follow the path for about twenty minutes through a rolling gentle landscape along a valley.

Figure 8.9. Late Bronze Age warrior stela in Badajoz Museum

The dolmen has been consolidated after some destruction in the early 20th century, it was declared a national monument in 1957 it is one of the best examples of the Anta type of tomb. Along the path and at the tomb there are several information boards in both Spanish and English.

The circular chamber and entrance passage are all constructed from local granite. The covering mound, which has now largely gone, was shown by excavation to have consisted of layers of earth and pebbles from the nearby stream. It was elliptical and measured 35x28 metres and was probably six to seven metres high with kerb stones around the outside, some of them decorated (although now very difficult to see).

The passage ends in an entrance vestibule which is approximately six metres long with door jambs before entering the chamber. This is five metres in diameter and has seven massive stone uprights still in place. It is thought that the circular chambers of these Anta-

Figure 8.10. Dolmen del Prado de Lácara

type tombs could have had corbelled roofs although evidence for this is sparse due to subsequent damage. Along the passage and entrance vestibule some of the massive capstones are still in position.

Excavation in 1957 suggests that it could have been in use as a burial chamber for a thousand years. One skeleton in the foetal position had a range of grave goods including a necklace and a collection of fine flint arrowheads now on display in Badajoz Museum (see above). It dates to the Late Neolithic/Chalcolithic periods, approximately 2,500 BC to 2,000 BC.

Dolmen de Magacela (Dolmen de la Cerca del Marzo)

Unrestricted access

East of Mérida for approximately 40km along the N430, turn south and go through Villanueva de la Serena. Back roads will take you southwards to Magacela where the dolmen is signposted off the EX348.

This dolmen is badly damaged with the entrance passage and covering cairn all but gone. It is however remarkable for the engravings on the insides of several of the still extant chamber orthostats. The chamber consists of 12 granite uprights approximately 1.75 metres high giving a chamber diameter of 5 metres. The entrance is flanked by two larger stones 2m high. Of the 12 stones five show carvings on the inside faces although most are difficult to see.

Looking in from the entrance the stones are numbered from the left clockwise:

Stone number four is the most decorated with the carvings easiest to see. At the top right is an eleven-ray sun motif approximately 24cm in diameter. On

Figure 8.11. Dolmen de Magacela

the right is a 41cm x 24cm vertical feathered motif with a cup mark at the top and bottom. This is unique among megalithic engravings from the Iberian Peninsula. In the centre at the bottom of the stone is a 54cm long horizontal wavy snake-like motif that points towards a cup mark. There are several other cup marks between 3cm and 8cm in diameter at the bottom of the stone.

Stone number 6 has cup marks up to 10cm in diameter, some with attached grooves up to 55cm long.

Stones 7 and 9 have carvings but they are impossible to see.

Stone 8 has a 31cm by 19cm oval depression at the top, a feathered motif similar to stone 4 but in a horizontal position with cup marks at the top and bottom of it and a nearby hook motif.

Dolmen Sierra Gorda

Unrestricted access

This dolmen is 20 kilometres south of the Dolmen de Magacela (above). It is signposted from the EX345 just north of Valle de la Serena, on the right if going north. There is about 2km of a fairly rough track to reach the site which is in a walled enclosure at the back of a farm building at the end of the track.

The dolmen is in moderately good condition and there is an information board (in Spanish) which includes drawings of some of the artefacts discovered during excavation. These include beads, pottery and an interesting, decorated stone plaque.

Many stones of the covering circular cairn survive with evidence for the original kerbstones in places, approximately 12m in diameter. The corridor is six metres

Figure 8.12. Dolmen Sierra Gorda

Figure 8.13. Dolmen de la Granja de Toriñuelo

long and together with the circular chamber is constructed of orthostats, the latter having 22 uprights the tallest being 1.2m. According to the information board two of the orthostats are decorated but we failed to find them.

Dolmen de la Granja de Toriñuelo

Restricted access

Ask at the Tourist Office in Jerez de los Caballeros, 1, Plaza San Agustín.

The town of Jerez de los Caballeros is south of Badajoz on the N345 and the dolmen is approximately six kilometres east of this on the EX112. The tomb is situated within the La Granja estate and access must be arranged through the tourist office, well worth doing as this is an impressive dolmen which has been extensively reconstructed. Although parts of the reconstruction are unrealistic to be able to see and be inside a fairly complete tomb does give a completely different feel to looking at other dolmen which lack lintel stones and rooves.

The site was declared a national monument in 1926 and is a good example of the Anta (or Tholoi) type of tomb with a long passage leading into a circular chamber with a corbelled stone roof which here is nearly complete. The chamber is about 3.6m diameter and is constructed of thirteen orthostats, three of which are decorated with a variety of serpentine, circular and radial motifs. One free standing stone has a wonderful human face with a complicated head dress arrangement and possible belt. It is suggested that some of the orthostats would have been painted as well as carved. The corbelled stone roof is mostly reconstructed but gives a good impression of what it must have been like originally.

The tomb is oriented east-west and has an access corridor 25m long, over one metre high, the upper levels of which have been partially reconstructed although the orthostats are in their original positions. The enclosing mound is mainly in place and has a diameter exceeding 70m, excavation having shown that it is constructed from alternating layers of clay and stones.

Figure 8.14. The chamber of the Dolmen de la Granja de Toriñuelo

Dolmen de Huerta Montero

Restricted access

This must be one of the most informative presentations of a dolmen anywhere in Spain. It has been extensively excavated and is now housed within an interpretation centre. Visits are organised through the tourist office (in the middle of town by the church) who may provide an English-speaking guide, Almendralejo tourist office, 16, Pl. Iglesia.

The site is in the suburbs of Almendralejo, about 25km south of Mérida along the A66. It was discovered in the 1990s and excavated over three years mainly by local volunteers. The covering building was completed and opened in 2011 providing an integrated information centre together with preservation for the exposed remains. Around the walls are large information panels (in Spanish but with very good graphics) explaining the landscape around, the structure of the tomb and the burials and grave goods within.

Figure 8.15. The structure of Dolmen de Huerta Montero

This tomb is unusual in being dug into the ground rather than having orthostats above ground level. It is in three sections: a stepped ramp going downwards about seven metres long; a corridor of orthostats four metres long and then the circular chamber of 4.6m diameter which originally would have had a corbelled roof, now gone. One very unusual feature of this tomb is that the walls of the chamber are plastered with a lime-based rendering and evidence for the manufacture of this is nearby. Around the chamber are three pits showing where limestone was crushed and mixed with water to produce the rendering which was plastered around and over the orthostats.

Excavation revealed a remarkable level of detail, not only of the structure itself but also of the burials within the chamber. This is very unusual as normally dolmen chambers have been robbed or destroyed so little is known compared

Figure 8.16. Dolmen de Huerta Montero

Figure 8.17. The chamber of Dolmen de Huerta Montero

to the wealth of detail here. Radiocarbon dating has shown that there were two phases of burial within the chamber, the first dating to approximately 2,600 BC. The bones of 75 individuals were identified of which 42 were adults with an average age of 23 years. The information boards on the walls around the tomb give lots of detail of the burials and grave goods with very good drawings. Of special interest are the four complete skeletons buried in the foetal position. The artefacts include bones with incised decoration including a whistle made from an ostrich bone decorated with a face and skirt.

The second phase of burial is approximately 1,000 years later and grave goods include much better made and decorated pottery than in the first phase. Analysis of some of the human teeth showed that they were enjoying a diet of cereals, meat and acorns, and some of the worn knee bones of the women suggest that they were spending a lot of time kneeling, perhaps grinding cereals on a saddle quern. Some of the finds are in Badajoz Museum (see above).

The passage is aligned to allow the sun at sunrise on the winter solstice to shine along it and into the chamber. Lines of postholes around the chamber show how the builders set out the alignment before constructing the tomb. This is brilliantly demonstrated by a series of spotlights that simulate the moving sun and shine along the passage and illuminate the rear wall of the chamber. It may be that this is a common feature with tombs that have entrance passages and has certainly been demonstrated as far away as Newgrange in central Ireland.

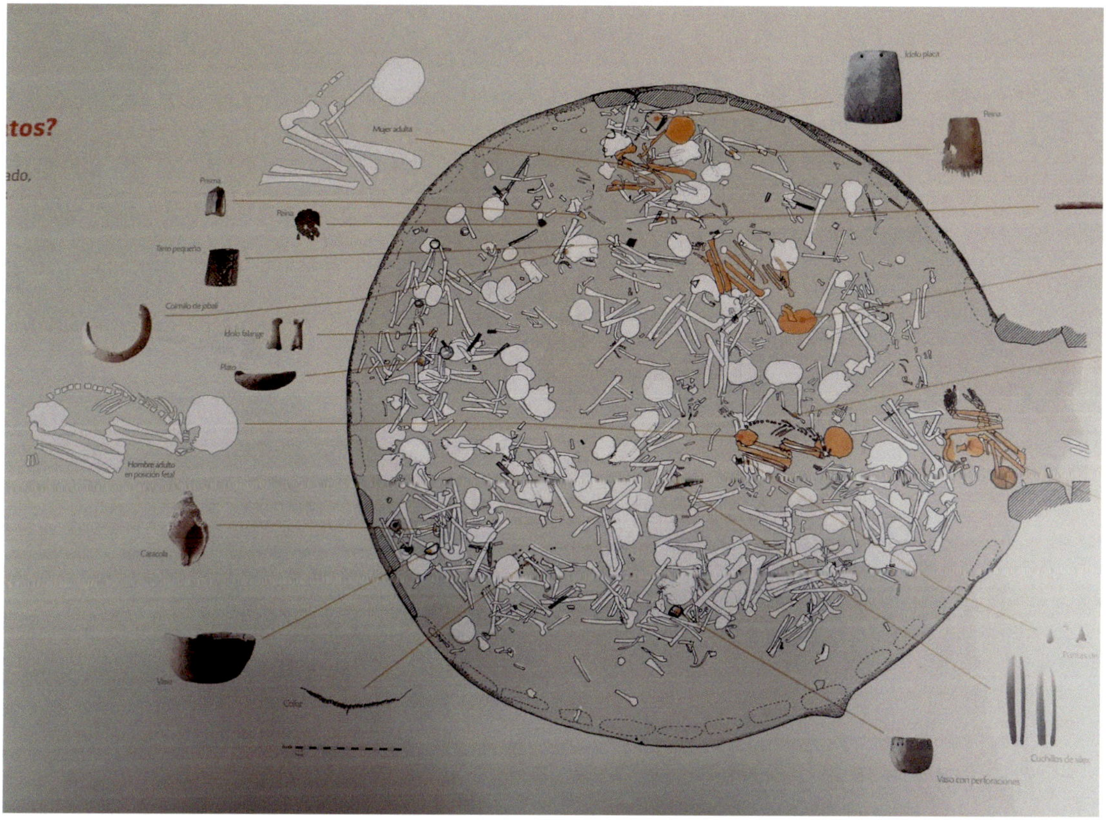

Figure 8.18. A display board at Dolmen de Huerta Montero showing the distribution of human bones and artefacts within the chamber

One of the problems with the late Neolithic/Chalcolithic period is the lack of known settlements compared to the large number of burial monuments. On a hilltop a few kilometres from this tomb is a settlement shown by small-scale excavation to be contemporary with this tomb. It is surrounded by three stone-built walls and has the remains of stone houses inside. Unfortunately, the site is entirely neglected, difficult to find and, therefore, not worth visiting although our Tourist Office guide did take us there so try asking.

Andalucia

EXTREMADURA
CASTILE - LA MANCHA
N
W
E
S
PORTUGAL
CÓRDOBA
SEVILLE
HUELVA (M)
(I)
GRANADA
(M)
ANTEQUERA
MÁLAGA
(M)
ALMERÍA
MEDITERRANEAN SEA
NORTH AFRICA
Petroglyph
Dolmen
Settlement
(M) Museum
(I) Interpretation Centre

Chapter 9
Andalucía

Andalucía is one of Spain's largest autonomous regions with wonderful cities, villages, mountains, beaches and rolling countryside. The archaeology is equally as diverse and interesting ranging from prehistoric monuments to 8th/7th century BC Phoenician trading colonies along the Mediterranean coast, to being one of the Roman Empire's most important and wealthiest areas, to the delights of Islamic Spain occupied from AD 711 until the 15th century. Here we concentrate on a very small proportion of the rich prehistoric heritage in these areas – north of the coastal town of Huelva, the town of Antequera which is just north of Málaga, around the village of Gorafe which is north-east of Granada and Almería.

The focus here is on dolmen with some of the largest and best examples in the whole of Spain plus a remarkable prehistoric settlement.

North of Huelva

Before visiting the dolmen described below it is worth going to the museum in Huelva which contains archaeology from the Palaeolithic to medieval periods. It has some detailed information on the sites below as well as much background material.

The Museum of Huelva

Alameda Sundheim, 13
Restricted access

This museum is housed in a very attractive building with beautiful gardens on one of the main streets in Huelva. It is unusual and interesting because it focusses on the theme of mining and metalworking through the ages. This is unsurprising because not far north are the mineral rich areas of the Río Tinto and the massive mines which are still operating today. The museum is on two floors and contains an art collection.

Within 40km north and east of the town of Huelva are two groups of dolmen, El Pozuelo and Los Gabrieles and a single, massive tomb known as the Cueva del Zancarrón de Soto, or just Soto. If you are short of time then Soto is the most spectacular, and one of the few with megalithic art, although this is heavily reconstructed and subject to opening hours. If you have half a day to spare then the Pozuelo group are relatively easy to find and very rewarding with several having been excavated and reconstructed. The Gabrieles group are more difficult to find and in a much poorer state of preservation although in a nice area for walking.

Cueva del Zancarrón de Soto (Dolmen de Soto)

Restricted access

The dolmen is signposted left from the minor road, the A472 from Huelva towards La Palma de Condado, just after crossing over the main A49 road. The unmade track is several kilometres long and very bumpy. There is supposedly another way to the dolmen from the town of Trigueros taking the Calle Sevilla for about 8km although we cannot verify this route.

The tomb was discovered by Armando Soto, a local antiquarian, and then excavated by the German archaeologist Hugo Obermaier in the 1920s. It was declared a national monument in 1931 and is the largest and most important of over two hundred dolmen known in the province of Huelva. At the entrance to the fenced compound is a notice board with a brief description in English, everything else around the site is in Spanish only. This monument will not be to everyone's taste as it is heavily reconstructed but is probably one of the biggest dolmen you will see anywhere and it does have some very nice art on the passage uprights. On the way to the tomb entrance is a small sunken interpretation centre with some limited information on dolmen in Andalucía and megalithic art.

Based on the excavated evidence it seems that the tomb itself was preceded by a Neolithic stone circle which was then replaced by the 80m diameter low cairn making it one of the largest tombs in Europe. The cairn has revetting kerb stones, some of the originals being preserved. The building of the cairn is dated to between 2,500 BC and 2,000 BC by radiocarbon dating, the Chalcolithic period. There is one 21m long passage varying in width from approximately 1m

Figure 9.1. The Dolmen de Soto

Figure 9.2. The passage of the Dolmen de Soto

to 3m, it has a wider antechamber at the entrance and ends in a single chamber. All of the uprights and capstones are in place creating a very atmospheric experience as you walk along the passage. Although the chamber had been plundered eight crouched skeletons with grave goods were found during the excavations. Within and around the entrance antechamber excavation showed postholes, structures and evidence of various sorts of what is claimed to be ritual activities associated with the burial ceremonies.

Other than its sheer size, what makes Soto very special is the art. The passage is dimly lit so that as you walk along it you can make out various pecked and incised human figures, symbols and patterns on many of the upright stones. As with many megalithic structures of all kinds, dolmen included, their orientation is central to interpreting and understanding them. Soto is oriented east-west and at the spring and autumn equinox the first rays of the morning sun shine along the passage and illuminate the chamber.

Dolmen del Pozuelo

Unrestricted access

The village of El Pozuelo is signposted from the N435 about 8km north of Valverde del Camino. The dolmen are in two groups, tombs 1 to 4 and tombs 5 to 9. As you approach the village there is a sign to an unmade road on the left which leads to dolmen 1 to 4, about 4km. Straight on leads to a signed road to the right which goes to dolmen 5 to 9, about 2km. We suggest that you visit 5 to 9 first.

There are 11 tombs in total in this area and they are important because in the late

Figure 9.3. Art in the passage of the Dolmen de Soto

1990s many of them underwent a programme of excavation, conservation and reconstruction. This makes them very accessible and informative, many of them have information boards and they are numbered. Unfortunately, some of the display boards are in poor condition and the tombs are not well maintained, another sad victim of Spain's ailing economy since 2008. A range of artefacts were excavated from tombs 3, 5 and 6 including different forms of pottery, stone tools and beads, all dating to between 3,000 BC and 2,500 BC. Some of these are now on display in the Museum of Huelva together with a wider explanation of the tombs themselves.

Just before the village take the turning to the right signposted to the dolmen, after about 2km you will reach a car park with a large display board in poor condition. Take the path to the left, following the green and white posts, and within a few minutes you will reach Tomb 6 on a slight hill.

Tomb 6 is the most interesting of the whole El Pozuelo complex because of its unusual and complex structure and because it has been extensively excavated and reconstructed. The reconstruction has created a section through the cairn so that the original size and form of it can be imagined. Here you can see the large flat kerbstones that are keyed into the cairn itself. The tomb is an unusual converging corridor design with four chambers, two to the right and two to the left bifurcating from a single entrance. The reconstruction has replaced all the uprights and the capstones on the chambers.

Figure 9.4. Dolmen del Pozuelo Tomb 6

Figure 9.5. Dolmen del Pozuelo Tomb 5

Return to the car park and take the path the other side of the main display board, Tomb 5 is about a 30-minute walk along this track through nice woodland. After a few minutes, just over a small bridge, ignore the sign to the left to Dolmen 5 and 8, keep going along the track. Turn left at the T-junction, pass some ruined reconstructed round houses on the left (we have no idea what these were meant to be for), Tomb 5 is further on on the left. There is an information board in Spanish. This is also a corridor tomb with four chambers, one of which has capstones, and an antechamber at the entrance. The cairn is about 19m in diameter, an average size for the El Pozuelo group. There is a sign to Tomb 8, 350m, but this has not been conserved and there isn't much to see even if you can find it.

From Tomb 5 you can continue along the track to the other group, Tombs 1 to 4, about 2km distance or return to the car park and drive there.

If you return to the car park just before you reach it on the left is a signed path to Tomb 7. This is on a hilltop with a fantastic 360-degree view. It is a passage tomb with three chambers and has been restored, there is an information board in Spanish. All uprights are in place and two capstones.

Just as you leave the car park, on the left is Tomb 9 with an information board. There isn't much left of this one although some of the cairn is visible together with some uprights of what was originally a corridor tomb with a single chamber.

For Tombs 1 to 4 return to the road you came in on and take the other signed track, continue along it until you reach a building on the right hand side (there is a path to the left which goes to an old mine, visible on the hilltop), just past the building on the right hand side is a signposted track to Pantano El Vela. Park here and on the other side of the road are two marked paths, one to Tombs 3 and

Figure 9.6. Dolmen del Pozuelo Tomb 7 (© Ángel M. Felicísimo)

4 and one to Tombs 1 and 2. All four are close together and can be seen in the middle distance from here on low hills.

Tomb 1 has a well-preserved cairn and kerbstones some of which are quite high but have been restored, it is a corridor tomb with two chambers. Many of the uprights are in position but there is only one capstone. Tomb 2 is a cruciform tomb so it has a long passage and two side chambers at the end which are quite badly damaged, this one hasn't been conserved and restored. It has very distinctive flat angled kerbstones in places around the cairn. This seems to be a construction technique particular to this area and can be seen on other El Pozuelo tombs. There is a good view of Tombs 3 and 4 from here, both of which have been restored and are a short walk away.

Figure 9.7. Dolmen del Pozuelo Tomb 1

Tomb 3 is a corridor tomb with two chambers, most uprights are in place with a single capstone. The cairn is very well preserved nearly to the height of the uprights. Tomb 4 is a different form of corridor tomb with a large chamber with a central division. Both of these have flat angled kerbstones.

Dolmen de los Gabrieles

Unrestricted access

About four kilometres out of Valverde de Camino on the A493 to La Palma de Condado is a large brown sign on the left indicating an unmade track, take this. Note that this was once a well-marked route with all six dolmen signposted but it is now very neglected and we found only the remains of signs with no information thus making it difficult to find the sites. We in fact only found three of the six but only spent an hour or so looking. Even so it is an interesting landscape of oak woods and some agriculture which provides good walking, and the dolmen are worth seeing if you can find them!

Continue along the track for approximately four kilometres, you will see the remains of the wooden signs, follow these and at an obvious fork with a ruined sign take the left route. The track will end with a ruined building on the right and an unusual circular low building which we subsequently found out is called a zahúrda, a pigsty.

Of the three tombs that we found the preservation varied and all dated to the Chalcolithic period, 2,500 BC to 2,000 BC based on limited excavation at a couple

Figure 9.8. One of the Dolmen de los Gabrieles

of the sites. The track ends at one tomb, not far from the building. This has the uprights of a passage leading to a chamber, a small chamber off to the right has capstones. A couple of hundred metres back along the track is another tomb, on the right as you walk back. This also has a long passage and single end chamber consisting of only uprights. One curious feature of this tomb are the big kerb stones at the entrance suggesting a more complex original design. A little further along the track is a third dolmen which is in poor condition with only a few uprights of the passage left. According to our information there are two more dolmen worth seeing in this group, one along a track to the right and the other along a track to the left before you reach these three. We didn't find them either.

Antequera

The three dolmen on the outskirts of Antequera are very impressive due to their size, quality of preservation and their excellent interpretation centre. For background contextual information it is worth visiting the Museum of Antequera in the town centre as well as the town itself. One of the highlights is the Islamic Alcazaba with spectacular views and a very interesting self-guided tour.

The Museum of Antequera

Plaza Coso Viejo
Restricted access

The museum is located centrally and has its origins in the small archaeological museum started in 1908 by local archaeologist Rodrigo Amador de los Ríos. In 1966 it was moved to its present location, the Nájera Palace which was refurbished and expanded in 2009. The result is a majestic building which combines the traditional courtyard house with large modern gallery space. The prehistoric collection is in the first rooms on the ground floor covering the Palaeolithic to the Iron Age. The displays are well organised and presented with English as well as Spanish explanations. One nice touch is that individual and groups of artefacts are interpreted by practices, so for example, pottery production, metalworking and burial.

Dolmen de Viera, Menga and El Romeral

Restricted access

All three of these tombs are located about 1km from the city centre to the northeast and are signposted. We recommend that you visit Viera and Menga first which will include a visit to the interpretation centre.

These are three of the most impressive tombs in Spain and together with their surrounding landscape have been a World Heritage Site since 2016. This is one of the best examples of the importance of orientation being the reason for the positioning of dolmen passages. Menga is orientated towards a striking mountain called La Peña de los Enamorados which looks like a reclining human face in outline, this is northeast, a unique orientation for Iberian megaliths. Viera is pointing towards the equinox sunrise and El Romeral towards another very distinctive mountain on the horizon, El Torcal, again this is a very unusual direction being to the southwest. This relationship was first suggested in 1851 when Louisa Tenison visited Menga and recognised its orientation with La Peña. Much later in 2002 the Cambridge archaeologist Michael Hoskin drew attention to the exceptional Antequera tombs in his work looking at thousands of megalithic alignments across Europe. The tombs themselves have been known for a long time, probably due to their size and proximity to the city, Menga was first mentioned in a text of 1530.

The reception and interpretation centre shows an animation video of the building of one of the tombs, it is very well done and an excellent description of the logistics of moving such huge stones. The path then leads up to the Michael Hoskin Solar Centre which shows the skyline and the positions of sunrise at the solstices and equinoxes and how they relate to the tombs. The path continues to Viera and then Menga both of which were excavated between 1986 and 1995 and reconstructed, including their covering circular cairns both of about 50m diameter.

Viera is a corridor tomb of 22m long, about 2m high, 1.3m wide for most of its length but widening slightly to 1.6m at the end chamber. The corridor would have originally had 16 orthostats and 15 survive on the left-hand side and 14 on the right, five of the possibly 11 original roof slabs survive. On some of the uprights there are circular cupmarks, pecked indentations which are a common

Figure 9.9. Dolmen de Viera

Figure 9.10. The 'doorway' within Dolmen de Viera

feature of megalithic art. One interesting, and unusual, feature is at the end of the corridor the chamber is entered through a rectangular 'doorway' cut through a stone which is one of four forming the square chamber with a single capstone.

As you walk round to Menga it is worth noticing the position of these two tombs, on a high point overlooking a wide and fertile valley surrounded by mountains. Extensive archaeological work in the area has identified a number of Neolithic and Chalcolithic settlement sites, including caves with rock art, in the area which must form part of the same social system from which the people who built and used the tombs belonged to.

Figure 9.11. Dolmen de Menga

Figure 9.12. The interior of Dolmen de Menga

Menga is a completely different design to Viera and evidence suggests that it is earlier, perhaps dating to the Late Neolithic, 3,800 BC to 3,400 BC. It has an impressive atrium consisting of just orthostats which leads into a rectangular gallery which then leads into a huge oval shaped chamber. The overall length is 27.5m and at its highest 3.5m and its widest 6m. Each of the sides is made up of 12 orthostats with one massive one at the back, there are five massive roof slabs and three central stones supporting them. It is worth noting how accurately the massive slabs of the uprights and the roof stones fit together with hardly any gaps between them, a truly remarkable achievement. The first uprights of the gallery on the left have some pecked cruciform shapes and a star which could be prehistoric or, as some have suggested, medieval. Excavation has revealed a well at the back of the chamber, 1.5m diameter and 20m deep, probably dug during the 19th century. This shows that the tomb was open then and there are records of it being used as a holy place through the medieval period.

Leave the car park turning left and follow the signs to El Romeral, 2km away. This is a completely different type of tomb, sometimes called a tholos in reference to similar corbelled tombs in Greece. There has been no excavation here, although it has been conserved and reconstructed, and therefore there is no dating but is likely to be later than both Menga and Viera and date to the Chalcolithic of 2,500 to 2,000 BC.

El Romeral does not use massive upright orthostats but instead a technique of dry-stone walling on which the capstones are placed. It has an entrance atrium

Figure 9.13. The interior of Dolmen El Romeral

which leads to a passage ending in a circular dome chamber which then leads to a short passage and a smaller domed chamber. The passage is 26.3m long, 1.5m wide and 2m high. The large chamber is 5.2m diameter at ground level with vaulted dry-stone walls ending in a single cap stone, 3.75m high. The smaller chamber reproduces the larger one and the total length of the structure is 34m. The access doors to both chambers have orthostats rather than being dry stone walling. The circular cairn is truly massive at 85m in diameter. As you leave the tomb notice the avenue of cypress trees leading from the entrance and showing the alignment on El Torcal, the highest point of the distant mountains.

Gorafe, northeast of Granada

The village of Gorafe is signposted from the A92N between Guadix and Baza, on the GR 6100. The area around Gorafe is fascinating, not only for the number of dolmen here but also because the landscape, scenery and views are very special. This is Bad Land country where the River Gor has carved a wide and spectacular valley through soft rocks resulting in eroded ravines, gullies and canyons. Within the village and around are dwellings carved into the soft rock. The whole area is a Geological Park as well as a Megalithic Park and its stark beauty makes it of great interest. This is one of the greatest concentrations of dolmen in Spain with 242 having been located in 11 different 'cemeteries', more than 60 having been restored and can be visited via three marked trails. These are relatively small dolmen and many of them only retain their uprights and outlines of the cairns but what is remarkable is the density of tombs and how close together they are. Visiting them also provides very nice walking with some stunning views.

The dolmen of Gorafe were first studied in 1868 by Manuel de Góngora y Martínez and by the end of that century several of them had been excavated. During the 20th century more were discovered and by 1959 the 242 now known about had been described and classified into various types. The Megalithic Park was established in 2011 with the building of the Interpretation Centre and the establishment of the trails. Artefacts from the excavated tombs are in Granada museum and also in the National Archaeological Museum in Madrid indicating the importance of this collection of tombs which date to the late Neolithic and Chalcolithic periods, 2,500 to 2,000 BC.

The Interpretation Centre

Restricted access

This should be visited first, it is signposted in the village and not far from its centre. The building is futuristic and is supposed to resemble a dolmen, it houses some surprising high-tech displays. Here you can get a map of the trail routes with tombs marked (they are all numbered) as well as other leaflets and information. There are also three films available to watch, two in Spanish and one in English, and it takes about an hour to watch these and have the guided walk around the Centre. The first film describes life in the Neolithic in the Gor valley, hunting, farming, religion and ritual and shows a typical settlement of the time. Another room has a display which details the history of discovery of the megaliths as well as describing the different types, for example gallery and passage. The second film is watched from a spiral ramp looking down onto a large glass dome onto which the images are projected. This covers the building of a dolmen in detail from laying out the plan, quarrying and moving the stones and constructing the covering cairn. As said, these are relatively small dolmen but still involve stones weighing 10 tons or more which would take many people to move.

The final room has an interesting interactive map of the area that the guide uses to explain the geology as well as the different megalithic routes. There is also a film, in English, on Megaliths in Andalucía. This gives a thorough coverage of the development of megaliths throughout Europe, starting in the 5th millennium BC and reaching the zenith in the 3rd millennium. It gives a good explanation of the different types of megaliths, not just dolmen, and suggests that Andalucía is important as the area where the spread of the two major types met. These are the gallery type dolmen from the Atlantic zone and the tholos passage graves from the Mediterranean area (see above, El Romeral, Antequera for a tholos tomb). In a final room is the funerary stele from dolmen 77, one of only two known in Andalucía. Engraved on its surface, although difficult to see due to weathering, is a human figure with a headdress with three feathers and a cane in its right hand. Also in this room is a display of stone tools with their modern equivalents.

The dolmen that can be visited are along three routes, these can be done in any order, if you are short of time the first route described below is the easiest and includes Tomb 134 which is one of the best preserved.

Ruta las Hoyas del Conquín

Unrestricted access

Take the road back up the valley from Gorafe, after the deserted farmhouse on the left is a car park on the left with the Megalithic Park sign. The ruta is in two parts, Alto above the road, Bajo below the road. At the car park is Tomb 135 with a small chamber and a few uprights of the passage. Take the path upwards to Tomb 134 which is well preserved with an entrance atrium and portal stone, and a single chamber. The uprights are embedded in bedrock which is unusual and two large capstones are still in place. Further up the path and close together are three more. Number 133 has a small single chamber with a capstone, 132 has a single square chamber and short passage. Number 239 is of a different design with a single square chamber and no obvious way in or out.

Figure 9.14. Dolmen de Gorafe, Tomb 134

Return to the car park and cross the road where the path provides a nice walk down into the valley. Tombs 137 and 138 both have a single chamber, short passage with only the uprights surviving. There isn't much left of 139 but 140 and 141 offer more complete chambers, the last with a doorway. Both of these groups show the main characteristics of the Gorafe dolmen as a whole – they are constructed from local rock, the hard bands within the valley sides, they are small but close together in cemeteries and there are subtle variations in design.

Figure 9.15. Dolmen de Gorafe, Tomb 141

Figure 9.16. Dolmen de Gorafe, Tomb 110

Ruta Llano de Olivares

Unrestricted access

Continue along the road up the valley to the car park at the top. This group of dolmen are strung out along the cliff top overlooking the Gor valley, you can drive along the trackway or walk. The views are magnificent with the often snow-capped Sierra Nevada to the left and other mountains in the distance. It is about 1km to the main concentration or 3km to see them all. The first three, 118, 117 and 116, are all very similar and not well preserved with just uprights. The main concentration is at the viewing point over the valley with a notice board which has an English explanation of dolmen. Here there are five very close together, 108 to 112, all very similar with just uprights. Further along the track are four more, 102, 103, 106 and 240, again very similar.

Ruta de Majadillas

Unrestricted access

The third group is on the other side of the river and can be accessed in two different ways. There is a walking track signposted from the road at the back of the Interpretation Centre, this crosses the river and carries on up to the dolmen.

Alternatively, you can drive by going along the GR6100 towards Baños de Alicún, turn left onto the GR 6101 just before the large spa hotel. The advantage of going this way is that you can see the rock carved petroglyphs which are the oldest in the province of Granada and well worth the effort. Just after the turning, on the right in some trees are two dolmen, there is a track with a chain across it. Numbers 11 and 12, both poorly preserved, although 12 has a capstone.

The petroglyphs of Cerro de la Mina

Unrestricted access

About 1km from the turn along the GR 6101 is a derelict building on the left, park here. Just before the building is a track on the same side, it has a chain across it but you can go around this. There are no signs to the engravings. Carry on upwards bearing right, at a T-junction, with a large, pitted boulder on the right, turn right. The gravel track zig-zags upwards for about a 30 minute walk, at the end where the gravel ends take the path to the left signed by small piles of stones. This will lead to four rounded large boulders on the left overlooking the valley with fabulous views. These are the engraved boulders and date to the Chalcolithic, 2,500 BC to 2,000 BC. The engravings are still quite deep and well preserved and show a variety of stylised human figures claimed to be male and female taking part in a ritual dance on the first two boulders. The third has a large sun with rays symbol and the fourth has a series of cup marks.

For the *Ruta de Majadillas* carry on along the GR 6101 for about 8km, signpost to dolmen on the left, follow the track and park at the end where another sign is. Walk to the right following the edge of the field and then down a track. To the left are dolmen 65, 66 and 67 and an information board. It has been noticed that the dolmen on this side of the river are generally bigger than those on the other side. Number 65 has a well-preserved big chamber with two capstones and a very interesting entrance portal stone. Nearby is dolmen 66 and 67, both with large uprights. Follow the signed path to the rest of this group, another 12 dolmen numbers 68 to 79. These are all very similar, number 71 is a good example

Figure 9.17. A part of the petroglyphs of Cerro de la Mina

Figure 9.18. Dolmen de Gorafe, Tomb 65

with a large square chamber consisting of seven uprights and a short entrance passage. Number 77 is where the funerary stele on display in the Interpretation Centre was found, positioned outside the entrance. Again, the importance of these is not the size and form of individual tombs but the concentration of them in a cemetery showing great cohesion in the burial rites of this community over a long period of time.

Almería and Los Millares

South of Granada is the coastal city of Almería, worth visiting in its own right but also because not far away from it is the very impressive prehistoric settlement of Los Millares, one of the most important Chalcolithic (Copper Age) sites in Spain and indeed Europe. Before going to the site we recommended that you visit the archaeological museum in Almería for a full background and much detail.

The Archaeological Museum of Almería

Carretera de Ronda/Calle Hermanos Pinzón
Restricted access

This is a very good, modern, high-tech museum with interactive displays in Spanish and English, especially good for children. The building is superbly designed as typified by the aerial display called Nube de Siret (Siret's cloud) which hangs from the ceiling of the entrance lobby and pays homage to Luis Siret who discovered Los Millares and conducted the first excavations there donating the finds to the original museum. A novel feature is the timeline, the stratigraphic column, which extends up the central staircase. The first floor and part of the second are devoted to the Chalcolithic and Early Bronze Age periods as represented by the two important local sites Los Millares and El Argar, the third and second millennia BC. The many finds from these sites are superbly displayed and explained. The whole range of material culture is shown from flint tools to pottery and copper objects. Although the focus is on these two sites, and Los Millares in particular, they are put into a wider regional context with information on other sites. You get a good idea of the way people lived, farmed and buried their dead five thousand years ago.

There is also very good use of models and reconstructions. The model of Los Millares at its zenith shows what a large and complex site it was with surrounding walls with towers, a large number of houses and the necropolis containing many tombs. The reconstructed tomb with skeletons positioned as found is particularly good with an audio-visual display of burial rites. There is also an informative display on the methods and techniques of archaeology.

Los Millares

Restricted access

Take the AL3411 through Gador north of Almería, Los Millares is signposted. This is a large site covering at least 5ha so give yourself plenty of time as there is much to see.

Information in Spanish and English is available at the entrance office and there are information boards positioned around the site as well as a good leaflet to go with them. There is also a very informative interpretation area within the site which has reconstructed roundhouses and other structures. Positioned within the surrounding landscape are a series of fortlets associated with the main settlement and also several dolmen. A map in the entrance office shows walking routes to get to these although the easiest is along a track on the opposite side of the road from the office. This is Fortín 1, which has two circular defensive walls

Figure 9.19. A model of the settlement of Los Millares

Figure 9.20. Reconstructed houses at Los Millares

with towers and a ditch 6m deep, it is worth visiting and also has tremendous views over Los Millares.

The site is situated on a triangular spur between two dry riverbeds. It was discovered in 1891 by the engineer Luis Siret during the construction of a railway line. He carried out the first excavations in the early twentieth century and they have continued spasmodically since. The site dates from between *c.* 3,200 BC and *c.* 2,300 BC and during this time underwent a series of changes. The area of occupation was extended three times resulting in four successive massive defensive stone walls with towers and embellished entrances, up to 4m high originally. The foundations of parts of these can be followed on the ground and the main gate of the fourth, outer, wall is particularly impressive having a massive barbican with towers. This is 310 metres long cutting off the entire spur and is the longest Copper Age wall in Europe. Not far from here an aqueduct goes through the wall carrying water to the settlement from a spring nearby. Within the enclosures are many roundhouses, the maximum population is estimated to be about two thousand people. These are 6m to 7m in diameter with stone-built walls, originally thatched rooves and pounded earth floors.

Although these days the landscape is very dry and arid 5,000 years ago it was much more amenable with forests and areas of agriculture and the River Andarax was navigable. The people hunted deer and boar, bred sheep, goats and pigs and grew cereals and vegetables. Their skill in making decorated pottery, copper tools and weapons, basketwork and intricate jewellery can be seen by the finds in the museum in Almería and also in the National Archaeological Museum in Madrid.

Figure 9.21. A tomb at Los Millares

Outside the living areas are groups of tombs, more than one hundred known in total. These are tholos or beehive tombs which originally had a corbelled stone roof the idea for which may have spread from the Aegean. The chamber is reached by a short passage with perforated slate slabs which you crawl through to gain access. Within the tombs, along with skeletons, were found grave goods of pottery, tools, weapons and enigmatic clay figurines or idols.

Catalunya
FRANCE
ANDORRA
FIGUERES
ROSES
(I)
(I)
GIRONA
LLEIDA
(I)
ARAGÓN
(M)
BARCELONA
TARRAGONA
N
E
W
S
Menhir
Dolmen
Rock Art (Rock Shelter)
Settlement
(M) Museum
(I) Interpretation Centre

Chapter 10
Catalunya

Catalunya's position in the northeastern corner of Spain gives it a very varied topography. Running along its northern borders with France are the spectacular Pyrenees with peaks of 3,000m and remote valleys which are favourite places for walkers, cyclists, skiers and climbers. The central and southern areas are lower and contain areas with different interests such as the wetlands of the Ebro delta. There are numerous historic cities including Tarragona, Lleida, Girona and Figueres the latter being one of two places to visit if you are interested in Salvador Dalí.

This area is probably more well known, however, for its beaches and seaside holiday places along the Mediterranean costas such as Lloret de Mar, Tossa de Mar and Roses. The other great attraction of course is the city of Barcelona with so much to see and do there although beware if you don't like mass tourism. With this in mind the sites we describe below are all just a few kilometres inland from the coast so they can be easily visited if you are on holiday there.

The Roca dels Moros or Caves of El Cogul rock art

El Cogul
Restricted access

The site and its visitor centre are situated on the outskirts of the small village of El Cogul, approximately 16km southeast of Lleida. Once at the village follow the signposts to *Arte Rupestre,* the visitor centre is an impressive new building.

This site is a rock shelter that contains rock art of the Levantine tradition which is found across a wide area of northeastern Spain (see page 89 for a full discussion). Before looking at the actual art it is essential to explore the visitor centre where good reproductions of the art are presented together with contextual explanations (in Spanish and English). The displays include some high-tech aspects including a downloadable multimedia guide and virtual reality headsets.

The site is in the fertile River Set Valley which has evidence for being occupied since Palaeolithic times and certainly through the Neolithic and Chalcolithic periods when much of the art is dated to. When first discovered in 1908 the rock shelter and its art were called the *Roca del Moros* as it was thought the Moors were responsible for it.

The centre piece of the interpretation centre is a life size facsimile of the rock shelter with the paintings. It is worth taking a good look at this as it is much clearer than the original. The rock has been painted many times so that the paintings represent a long period of activity. To the left are large animals which,

Figure 10.1. A tracing of the Dancers of Cogul (© Enric - CC BY-SA 3.0)

it is suggested may even be Palaeolithic while the main scene to the right is in the Levantine tradition. This shows forty-five human figures, of which thirty-eight are painted bright red, black and dark red, with seven being engraved into the rock face.

Within this larger scene are a group of nine red female figures dancing around a small black male figure with an abnormally large phallus. This scene, which gives rise to the whole being called the *Dancers of Cogul*, is explained on the surrounding displays and has been seen as a fertility/reproductive ceremony although more recently the interest has been on the relationship between the women figures. It has been suggested that these are women gathering to socialise with their children in a meeting place showing friendship and affection towards each other. Perhaps the paintings were done by women.

Inscriptions carved on the walls of the rock shelter (impossible to see in the original) are in Iberian script and Latin indicating that the place was used as a sanctuary into Iberian and Roman times.

Access to the original rock shelter is with a guided tour (in Spanish and Catalan). The art is difficult to see despite detailed conservation work by the Museu d'Arqueologia de Catalunya although some figures are visible and it is good to get a feel for the real place.

Figure 10.2. The Roca dels Moros

Signposted from the car park are the nearby *Saladar Tombs*. This is a cemetery of rock cut tombs which are worth a look if you have time although they are probably Moorish in date not prehistoric.

Castell d'Olèrdola

Sant Miquel d'Olèrdola
Restricted access

San Miquel d'Olèrdola is a small town about 10km inland from the popular holiday resort of Sitges. Take the C15 to the south of the town and then the BV-2443 at km 10 winding uphill to the Castell which is signposted. This is an impressive hilltop site with wonderful views in all directions largely surrounded by cliffs.

The site is part of the Archaeological Museum of Barcelona and was opened to the public in 1971 after extensive renovation work and excavation. Within the ticket Office is a small museum which details the chronological history of the hilltop which spans from the 8th century BC to the medieval period with excellent reconstruction drawings and a model of the hilltop. The site includes an Iron Age fortified nucleus, an Iberian settlement, a Roman fortification and a medieval town with Romanesque and pre-Romanesque churches and medieval tombs cut into the rock. As you walk around the hilltop there are information boards in English.

Figure 10.3. Paintings of animals in the Roca dels Moros

There isn't much to see here that is prehistoric - a reconstruction of a rock shelter with rock art and early Bronze Age Beaker pots in the museum, all found locally, although the Iron Age settlement is not visible. Even so this place rewards a visit because of the views and the quality of the archaeological evidence from later periods. The impressive main entrance and the walls constructed of massive polygonal blocks are Roman dating to the late 2nd century BC and replaced an earlier prehistoric wall of the 7th century. In the interior are a series of excavated Roman buildings including a huge rock-cut water cistern holding 350,000 litres of water with channels that fed it. At various places within the interior are excavated rectangular houses of the pre-Roman Iberian settlement, all well explained on the information boards. At the highest point is the magnificent church of Sant Miquel, started in 929 but rebuilt in the Romanesque style in the early 12th century, The church has been restored and one of its highlights is the decorated main door.

Figure 10.4. The Roman main entrance to the Castell d'Olèrdola

Dolmen de Pedra Gentil

Vallgorguina
Unrestricted access

Vallgorguina is an attractive small town east of Barcelona and about 8km inland from the coastal town of Arenys de Mar. It is situated on the C61, take exit 11 from the AP7-E15 or exit 19 from the C32. On the main street is a Tourist Information Office where information about this (in Spanish and Catalan) and other dolmen in the area can be gained.

To reach this site by vehicle when approaching from the AP7-E15 after about 4km take a right turn over a metal bridge where there is a sign for *Parc del Montnegre i el Corredor*. This leads to a dirt track which is dusty but fairly smooth and after about 2km there is a small car park and a short walk to the dolmen on the top of a small hill giving wonderful views. This really emphasises how carefully the location for dolmen was chosen to both give views outwards and to be seen from all around.

Figure 10.5. Dolmen de Pedra Gentil

The other way to reach the dolmen is on foot (we didn't do this so can't vouch for it). Carry on into Vallgorguina and turn right onto Carrer del Montseny where the houses start on the right. This leads to a car park where different walking trails start, follow the green and white one.

At the dolmen there is an information board (in Spanish and Catalan) with good details including illustrations of how a dolmen is

Figure 10.6. Menhir d'en Llach

constructed. This one is in very good condition and was reconstructed in 1855 as shown by the low wall around it. Much of the cairn material that would have covered it has gone. Its construction is relatively simple with seven uprights, three per side and one at the back, and a capstone giving a single chamber measuring about 3.5m by 2.5m.

The Paradolmen d'en Garcia

Unrestricted access

This site is in woodland approximately 6km inland from Tossa de Mar. Take the small GI681 road that runs inland from the coast road east of Tossa through Sant Grau, or southwards from the C35 at exit 95. At the 9km mark, on the right if going northwards, is an information board with a map and a place to park. Walk upslope into the woods following the good path marked in places as the 'Sender Mediterrani'.

This is a very nice walk across undulating terrain, notice the cork trees which have been harvested in the past. After about 15 minutes signed on the right-hand side the *Menhir d'en Llach*, a standing stone just over two metres high which appears to have been shaped with one side flat.

After about 40 minutes walking on the right is the paradolmen hidden behind a natural outcrop of rock, signed, walk around the back of this. Paradolmen are so called because they utilise natural rock outcrops as well as consisting of stones artificially placed, they are Neolithic burial chambers the same as the more usual dolmen. This one has two frontal uprights while the rear of the chamber is natural outcrop, the single capstone rests on both. Smaller boulders lying around could have been part of the original cairn.

Figure 10.7. Paradolmen d'en Garcia

Dolmen de Cova d'en Daina

Romanyà de la Selva
Unrestricted access

Romanyà de la Selva is a lovely small town about 8km inland from Platja d'Aro, just north-east along the coast from Tossa de Mar. Within a couple of kilometres east along the GIV-6612 the site is signposted on the left with a car park. There is an information board which describes a 4km circular walk taking in this dolmen plus another, a menhir and old churches. If you don't want to do this (we didn't) then Daina's Cave is 250m along the path.

This is an incredible dolmen, certainly one of the best preserved that we have seen anywhere in Spain. It was discovered in the late 19th century by local man Pere Cama i Casas, then excavated and partially reconstructed in the 1950s. It is positioned on a small hillock and constructed of massive granite blocks hewn from a local quarry. The uprights are positioned within holes and the capstones dragged into place over the surrounding stone cairn when it was built to the height of the uprights. It is Neolithic in date, 2,700 BC to 2,200 BC. This, and more, is explained on a good information board at the site (in several languages including English and Braille).

Figure 10.8. Dolmen de Cova d'en Daina

Figure 10.9. The entrance to Dolmen de Cova d'en Daina

This is one of the few dolmen where the shape and lower levels of the stone cairn which originally covered the chamber are preserved. The cairn is circular, about 11m in diameter, and kept in place by 37 kerbstones varying is size and shape but typically 0.5m to 0.75m high. Within these are the smaller stone boulders which make up the body of the cairn. There are seven and eight upright stones each side of the chamber and three surviving massive capstones. The internal rectangular chamber is approximately 7.6m long, 1.7m wide and 1.5m high. An unusual feature are the flanking stones at the entrance which seem to restrict access. The entrance is oriented southeast, it is argued to allow sunlight to enter the chamber on the winter solstice.

The excavations showed that this tomb was for collective burial with the bones and teeth of several adults and children being recovered. With the burials were a range of grave goods including pottery, flint tools and arrowheads, stone and gold beads. These are illustrated on the information board.

La Draga Neolithic settlement

Banyoles
Restricted access

Banyoles is 20km northwest of Girona. The La Draga Neolithic Park is out of town on the C-150a and it is signposted on the left. There is a large carpark for the lake and its activities, the Neolithic Park is on the lake edge, signposted. The lake is very attractive and has walking and cycling paths around it.

Note that there are two museums in the centre of Banyoles, both a few minutes' walk from the Plaça Mayor. The Darder Museum is natural history concentrating on the nearby lake. The Archaeological Museum (in Placeta de la Font, 150m along Carrer Major) contains information on the La Draga settlement and the Serinyà Prehistoric Caves described below, together with many artefacts. Unfortunately at the time of our visit (September 2024) this museum was closed for renovation but if you have time it would be worth checking. We were unable to establish when it would be reopening.

The La Draga early Neolithic settlement is important as being the only waterlogged lakeside settlement of that period in the Iberian peninsula. It was discovered in 1990 on the eastern edge of the lake and excavations have been ongoing since carried out by the Autonomous University of Barcelona, the Museum of Archaeology of Catalonia and the Centre of Underwater Archaeology of Catalonia. The Neolithic Park was established in 2000 to bring to life the Neolithic period through reconstructions and various activities.

Figure 10.10. Reconstructed Neolithic houses at La Draga

The site dates to the last quarter of the 6th millennium BC and its importance lies in the fact that it is waterlogged so organic materials are preserved as well as the usual materials such as pottery. These include bones, wood, fibres, textiles, seeds, leaves and even mushrooms. This enables not only a reconstruction of the village itself but also the surrounding environment around the lake.

The Park includes two reconstructed rectangular huts, longhouses, built on wooden piles to raise them above the boggy lakeside, hundreds of which were excavated in the lake by underwater archaeologists. The huts have wattle and daub walls and thatched rooves of reeds. In the huts are reconstructions of everyday Neolithic objects such as querns, pots and wooden tools. There are also displays of the range of cereals and plants grown and eaten in the period, as well as animals kept and fish caught in the lake. There are also display boards (in Spanish and Catalan) within the Park which explain these things. At weekends there are also activities for children such as how to make fire, how to knap flint and how to grind grain.

The Serinyà Prehistoric Caves Park

Serinyà
Restricted access

Turn left out of the La Draga car park on the C66, approximately one kilometre before Serinyà on the right is the car park to the caves, signposted. The Park was inaugurated in 1977 and the impressive interpretation centre was rebuilt in 2019 after flooding.

Here there are 13 caves, of which five can be visited and three have been extensively excavated. This is a key site for the Middle and Upper Palaeolithic of the Iberian Peninsula, with occupation related to pre-Neanderthal groups, about 250,000 years ago, Neanderthals (80,000 BC to 35,000 BC) and finally modern humans (Homo sapiens). The caves have produced a wealth of information about life in these early periods with some of the spectacular finds being: the oldest bone at 215,000 years ago, an adolescent from cave Mollet I; the oldest burial in Catalunya dated to 25,000 BC from cave Mollet III; the oldest musical instrument in Catalunya, also 25,000 BC, a bone flute from cave Pau II.

Start in the information centre where there is an interesting exhibition on early women archaeologists from the 19th and 20th centuries including Mary Leakey and Dorothy Garrod. In the same room is information on the excavations with some good old photographs of work in progress. In the other rooms are explanations (in Spanish and Catalan) of the geological formation of the caves in Travertine, a form of limestone. There are good graphics explaining evolution and the types of early Humans together with displays of flint and bone tools, also replicas of a Neanderthal and a modern skull for comparison.

The path outside takes you to the caves with each one being signposted, make sure you get an audio guide (available in English) which gives an excellent account of what was found where so it isn't necessary to repeat much here. The caves have access via steps with metal steps and walkways within them so that a good look around can be achieved.

In order of visit the caves are:

Figure 10.11. Cova de l'Arbreda

Cova de l'Arbreda. This had a roof originally which has collapsed. The excavated sections here are very impressive being tens of metres high and showing the stratigraphy through the excavated material. Towards the bottom are Middle Palaeolithic Neanderthal levels, 180,000 to 39,000 years ago, then the Upper Palaeolithic levels dating to 39,000 to 17,000 years ago and containing evidence for modern humans. These are mainly dated by flint and other stone tool types. There is also evidence for Mesolithic and Neolithic activity in this cave dating to 7,000 BC to 3,000 BC.

Cova de Mollet. This was one of the first to be excavated, starting in 1948 and ongoing. It has produced the earliest evidence, a tooth of Homo heidelbergensis dating to 250,000 to 200,000 years ago.

Cova del Reclau-Viver. This is the deepest cave for entering and has two rooms, a vestibule and a passage. Originally there were probably more. As well as Upper Palaeolithic material from here there has also been found Neolithic and Copper Age burials some dating back to 4,700 BC. There is also evidence for use of the cave in the Iron Age, from about 650 BC.

Overall, this set of caves demonstrate a remarkably long period of use from Middle Palaeolithic until Iron Age times. In the earlier periods they would have been used for temporary dwellings, the preparation and cooking of meat, together with some plants and berries. This is indicated by the range of stone tools, scrappers and blades etc. as well as animal bones and other environmental evidence. In the later periods, the caves seem to have taken on a more spiritual meaning to local people who were probably living out in the landscape and bringing their dead here to be buried.

Parc Megalític de Roses

Roses
Unrestricted access

It is advisable to visit the Tourist Information Office which is on the seafront in central Roses (Av. de Rhode, 77) where information on the Dolmen Trail and many other attractions is available.

From the seafront road towards the north of Roses, the Megalithic Park is signposted, then again to the right on the Carretera a Montjoi. After about 4km on the left are a couple of small parking places. There is a notice board which shows two walking routes, both with dolmen. We were advised that Route 1 was the best and we only did that one which takes in three dolmen and three menhirs. We took our time and it took us about three hours, it is circular. It is a lovely walk along some very attractive paths lined by dry-stone walls through what was obviously once a productive agricultural landscape with old field walls and olive groves. Based on the number of megalithic monuments in this area it must also have been well populated during Neolithic times.

The route does get rather vague in places, in theory you are following R1 which is shown on wooden posts along the way, some of the signs are in poor condition. Most of the monuments are off the main path and indicated on the posts but in very small writing! Halfway around R1 is a junction which takes you to R2, alternatively you can start R2 to the right of the car park. For R1 take the stone path uphill on the left of the car park. At the top of the hill, just past the ruined building on the right is the:

Dolmen de la Creu d'en Cobertella

Although surrounded by a wall and fence it is worth looking inside this monument and you can access it through the ruined building. This is a magnificent example of a dolmen, one of the largest and best preserved in Catalunya, constructed from massive stones from the local rock which is gneiss. In various places along the path you can see natural outcrops of bedrock which have weathered into flat slabs ideal for dolmen building.

Figure 10.12. Dolmen de la Creu d'en Cobertella

Figure 10.13. Dolmen de la Creu d'en Cobertella

There are three stones per side, two at the back and a huge capstone with wedge stones underneath. The entrance vestibule has door jambs which lead into the chamber and has a smaller capstone. The chamber measures 3.8m by 3.2m and is up to 2.5m in height, the large capstone is 5.65m by 4.10m by 0.40m.

Figure 10.14. Menhir de la Casa Cremada II

Carry on along the path, further on a junction can be ignored as the left hand path rejoins the right hand one. After about thirty minutes further on fork right after the ruined house and on the left is the:

Menhir de la Casa Cremada II

This vertical slab of gneiss is 2.35m high and for some reason, which is not at all obvious, it has a modern circular dry-stone wall around the base.

To the right you can take a short path to see the *Barroca de Pedra Seca*. This is a beautifully built, and probably reconstructed, dry-stone walled and corbelled roofed structure dating to the 17th or 18th century. The path drops down to the left and further on is an unnamed menhir on the right-hand side. Further along off to the right is a path to the:

Menhir de la Casa Cremada I

Figure 10.15. Menhir de la Casa Cremada I

This was discovered fallen over in 1996 and re-erected in 1997. It is a nice flat shaped piece of gneiss 2.4m high probably dating to the mid-late Neolithic period, 4th to 3rd millennium BC.

Continue along the main path and you come to a junction with Route 2 signposted to the right. As said, we didn't walk R2 but stayed on R1 where there are two more dolmen further on. Carry on past the modern house which will appear on the left, then on the right is the:

Dolmen del Llit de la Generala

This has been reconstructed with three side stones on each side, a rear stone and a single capstone. The circular cairn and suggested entrance passage are heavily reconstructed, and it is impossible to tell what the original looked like. This one (and the next one) are interesting in demonstrating the variation in size of dolmen. Comparing these with *Creu d'en Cobertella* (above) the design is very similar but the actual size of the stones used and the chamber enclosed are very different. It raises questions as to why – social status or serving the needs of different sized groups of people.

Figure 10.16. Dolmen del Llit de la Generala

A short walk further on the right is the:

Dolmen del Cap de l'Home

This is also small with just two side stones on each side, a rear stone and a capstone. In a beautiful position overlooking the Bay of Roses.

Figure 10.17. Dolmen del Cap de l'Home

From here the path home gets tricky. Retrace your steps past the last two dolmen and opposite the information boards, to the left of the house, is a scrubby narrow path which goes downwards. This will bring you down onto one of the main walled paths, turn left and head uphill eventually to reach the car park.

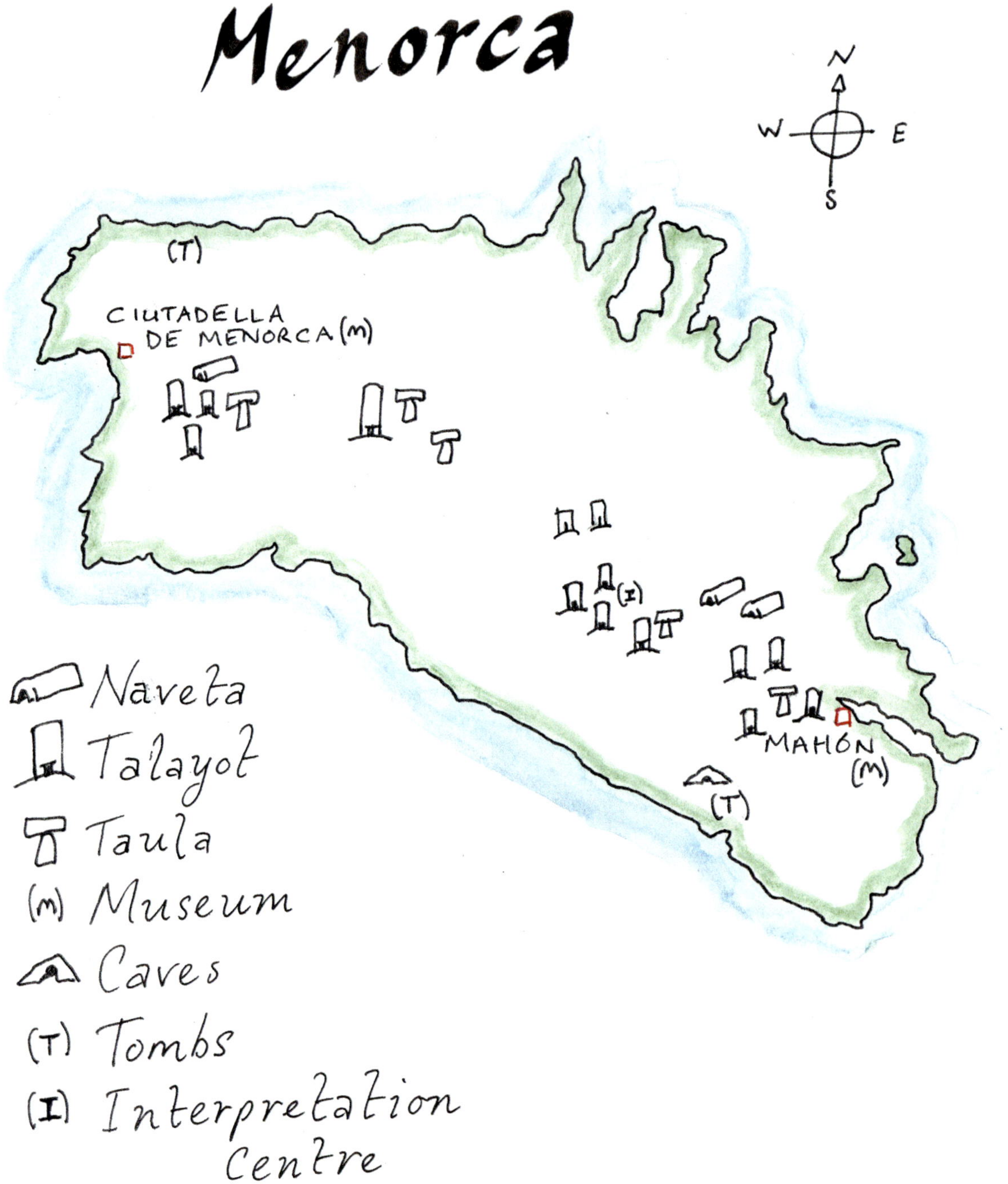
Menorca
N
W
E
S
(T)
CIUTADELLA
DE MENORCA (M)
(I)
MAHÓN
(M)
(T)
Naveta
Talayot
Taula
(M) Museum
Caves
(T) Tombs
(I) Interpretation centre

Chapter 11
Menorca

It is hard to summarise the attractions of Menorca, in many ways the most attractive of the Balearics. The northern half is more rugged with some moderately high hills while the southern half is a much gentler and rolling landscape of small walled fields. Much of the coastline is craggy with beautiful hidden beaches and coves. In 1993 Menorca was declared a UNESCO Biosphere Reserve indicating the importance of its natural heritage. As if this isn't enough reason to visit the island it also has the most incredible and unique prehistoric archaeology which must be seen to be believed. Here settlements and burial monuments are astounding and unlike anything anywhere else in Spain.

The prehistoric archaeology of Menorca

This is divided into three periods, each with its own types of structures:

The Pre-Talayotic period (sometimes called the Cave Era), dating from approximately 2,000 BC to 1,300 BC. Typical of this period are caves often used for burial and monumental structures known as Navetas. These are massive stone-built edifices resembling upturned boat hulls which were burial chambers and perhaps meeting places as well.

The Talayotic Period (or Bronze Age) from approximately 1,300 BC to 800 BC. Talayots are large stone-built towers usually found within settlements and may have acted as watch towers although why any one settlement would need more than one is unexplained.

The Post-Talayotic Period (or Iron Age) from approximately 800 BC to 100 BC when the Romans arrived. The characteristic feature of these settlements are the taulas which are large stone T-shapes with an upright and a large slab balanced on the top enclosed within a walled 'sanctuary'. It has been suggested that these may have been some form of altar although they remain a mystery as to their use and how people constructed them.

Of course, these date ranges are approximate and different features can occur within different types of sites, or the same site, if they are re-used over long periods of time. Some of the most significant sites are described below but there are many more scattered across the island, some you may come across are not well preserved and appear as a collection of enigmatic large stones. There are estimated to be around 1,500 prehistoric sites on Menorca with over 300 known talayots on the island.

Menorca has two main towns, the capital Mahón (Maó) in the east and Ciutadella in the west. Both have a museum containing prehistoric material and it is recommended that you visit at least one of these before seeing the sites, Mahón is the most comprehensive.

The Museum of Menorca

Carrer del Sol,
Plaça Pla des Monestir, Mahón
Restricted access

Housed in a very attractive and large 15th century building which was originally a Franciscan monastery. This museum covers the full history of the island from prehistoric to modern times. It has modern interactive displays, some in English, and is good for children. Some of the finest objects from the sites mentioned below are on display here including decorated pottery, stone and metal weapons and tools, jewellery together with background information and interpretation. There is a new immersive exhibition called Talayotic Menorca.

Some of the highlights for us are the artefacts that show everyday life and the often-underestimated skill and craftmanship of these past people. For example, the four pots found within a house at the Talayotic village of Torre d'en Galmés showing a wonderful state of preservation that is typical of the island, and incised decoration which is superbly crafted. Similarly, the perforated incense burner from Biniparratx Petit, the cheese-making pot from Trepucó and the polished bone punch from Cornia Nou found within a room with a whole assemblage of other tools dating to 800 BC to 600 BC. Perhaps the most enigmatic objects though are those associated with burial and religious beliefs. From the Cova (cave) de Mussol is an extraordinary human head looking upwards carved from olive wood, radiocarbon dated to *c.* 900 BC. Within one room at the Cova d'es Càrritx, of the same date, was a remarkable collection of 28 objects thought to be associated with preparing a body for burial including a range of vessels and implements as well as wooden and horn tubes filled with human hair.

The Municipal Museum

Bastió de sa Font, Ciutadella
Restricted access

Housed in an old fort which is worth seeing in its own right, although much smaller than the main museum it still holds a good collection of prehistoric material with some interesting objects. The displays are all in Catalan although there is an English leaflet available at the reception.

The road system of Menorca is fairly simple with a main road, the Me-1, going east to west from Mahón to Ciutadella with minor roads going off it to the north and south. Most of the sites described below are to the south and are signposted from the Me-1. Here we will describe sites approximately moving from east to west. If you are based in Mahón the first one, Trepucó, is a good one to start with as it is nearby and there is much to see there.

Taula and talayot de Trepucó

Camí vell de Sant Lluís
Unrestricted access

Situated within the southern suburbs of Mahón, take the Me-8 out of town, turn left at the roundabout onto Camí de Bintaufa, right onto Trepucó and right onto Camí Vell de Sant Lluís, there is a car park on the right.

This is one of the largest prehistoric villages in the Balearic Islands, covering an area of more than 5ha although only the areas of the taula sanctuary and the great central talayot can be seen. Because of its size it is thought to have been the centre of power in the east of the island. There has been considerable excavation here over the years, mainly in the 1930s by the British archaeologist Margaret Murray, with many finds displayed in the museum. In the late 18th century, the talayot was surrounded by the walls of a fort built during the Spanish siege of the island which was in British hands at the time. The 5-star shaped walls are still largely intact. Today the visible remains which have been partly restored are in three main areas, the large talayot, the taula enclosure and over to the west some houses and the surrounding settlement wall.

Figure 11.1. The Taula de Trepucó

Figure 11.2. The Talayot and houses of de Trepucó

The settlement was probably destroyed during the Second Punic War (218 BC to 201 BC) when General Magón (Hannibal's brother) took up residence in the port of Maó. It may be that the port and city could have taken their name from this event. It is thought that Magón was trying to recruit renown native sling-wielding warriors, called honderos, to fight against the Romans in Italy.

The oldest features are the two talayots the largest of which is 26m in diameter and still more than 8m high, there is also a much smaller one, both date to between 1,000 BC and 700 BC. Over to the west are a series of houses of the post-talayotic period, 650 BC to *c.* 200 BC which were enclosed by a wall of massive stones with square towers in the 5th century BC. The houses are multi-lobed with a central courtyard area and several rooms arranged around the outside. Also from this period is the taula sanctuary with its enigmatic structures suggesting that this was some form of religious/ritual enclosure kept separate from the domestic area.

Cornia Nou

Camí Vell de Sant Climent
Unrestricted access

On the western outskirts of Mahón, signposted right off the Me-12 along Sa Costa then turn right. This site is worth visiting because of the recent excavations and restoration work carried out by the Museum of Menorca. Many of the finds are on display in the museum.

The excavations concentrated on the talayot and an attached building and show important detail not known from other sites. The talayot is a large one and was constructed using a series of concentric walls with the gaps between infilled with stone. It has a flight of stone steps leading part-way up and some interesting internal layout including a corridor and a small room. The excavated building attached to it was probably used for grain processing showing evidence of roasting and grinding, it was radiocarbon dated to between 1,100 BC and the 6th century BC.

Talayot de Torelló

Camí Massupta Vell
Unrestricted access

Figure 11.3. The Talayot of Cornia Nou

The site can be reached from the Me-1, go south on the Me-14, right on the Me-12 then right on Massupta Vell, alternatively take the Me-12 out of Mahón.

Figure 11.4. The Talayot de Torelló

This is one of the biggest and best preserved talayots on the island dating to between 1,000 BC and 700 BC. Excavations around it have uncovered other areas of the surrounding village including some Roman occupation but there is nothing to see other than the talayot. Its diameter is 25m at the base and 22m at the top. It is unusual in having a doorway preserved towards the top with a stone lintel, the remains of a ramp leading up to the doorway can be seen. The large stones used to build this are of a remarkably regular size and shape showing the great skill of the builders.

Talatí de Dalt

Camí de Talatí
Restricted access

This site is about 4km outside Mahón along the Me-1, signposted to the left, there is a small car park. This is quite a large site to explore and there is a leaflet available at the entrance explaining the layout. There has been some excavation and it is estimated that the village was occupied for about 1,400 years and at its height in 300 BC about 100 people lived here.

The site has two small talayots and a large one of about 15m diameter although it is partially collapsed, all three have the remains of attached buildings. One of the highlights of this site is the ritual enclosure in the centre of the village, the taula sanctuary, horseshoe shaped and about 14m by 16m in size. Its surrounding wall is stone-built with occasional large upright stones. Inside is the massive well-preserved T-shaped taula and a smaller one which has toppled and is leaning against it. Excavation within this enclosure discovered the burnt remains of lambs and goat kids considered to be ritual sacrifices.

Figure 11.5. The taula at Talatí de Dalt

Another unusual feature of this site are the so-called hypostyle rooms. These are rooms built with columns holding up a roof of large stones. There are several at this site probably used for storage and dwellings at different times, the remains of one are next to the taula enclosure. There are also a couple of caves which were used for burials and within a grove of wild olive trees, so difficult to see, is a well.

Figure 11.6. A hypostyle room at Talatí de Dalt

Necropolis Cales Coves

Camí de Cales Coves
Unrestricted access

Take the Me-12 from Mahón to Cala en Porter, at about 10km turn left to Cales Coves, signposted. At the end of the road park and walk.

The main archaeological attraction here is nearly 100 burial caves cut into the cliff above the cove, some are visible from the cove. They span the periods from prehistory to Roman times but be warned that access is difficult, and some are hard to find. Even so it is worth visiting this beautiful cove where the swimming and snorkelling are very good.

There have been various periods of excavation of the tombs which are of different types. The oldest are natural caves with their entrances closed by stone blocks dating to between 1,100 BC and 700 BC. Between 800 BC and 600 BC artificial caves were dug and artefacts such as bronze torcs and weapons were deposited with the dead. In the Iron Age the artificial caves were bigger with supporting pillars which divided the internal space with iron knives, swords and bracelets being deposited together with some bronze objects. On the western side of the necropolis is a cave which was a Roman shrine in use during the 2nd and 3rd centuries AD with inscriptions dedicating it to the foundation of Rome.

Figure 11.7. Necropolis Cales Coves

Underwater excavation within the cove has identified a prehistoric and Roman jetty. To the west is another cove and beach which can be accessed by walking across the headland. Again this takes some searching for, but there is a talayotic period well dug into the bedrock with steps leading downwards.

Navetas de Rafal Rubí

Camí de Rafal Rubí
Unrestricted access

About 7km out of Mahón on the Me-1, turn right on Rafal Rubí, signposted. There is a car park. There are two tombs, each surrounded by a modern low stone wall.

These are the first navetas to see going east from Mahón and they are good examples of the type, well worth seeing, both have seen some excavation (finds exhibited in the Museum of Menorca) and restoration. These date to the pre-talayotic period, between 2,000 BC and 1,300 BC and are communal burial chambers and perhaps, also meeting places.

Navetas are constructed from huge stones (the so-called cyclopean technique) with an entrance in the façade leading into the inner chamber which is often divided into two levels, the rear end being apsidal in shape. Here the northern one is nearly 14m long with a maximum width of 9m, the façade is slightly concave and approximately 4m high. Some of the original structure has been destroyed and only five of the large roofing slabs survive. The entrance corridor is about 2.2m long giving access to the lower chamber through a perforated slab. A vertical corridor leads to an upper chamber. Excavation within the burial chambers found human skeletal remains together with pottery and bronze grave goods.

Figure 11.8. One of the Navetas de Rafal Rubí

The southern naveta is very similar but has a horseshoe-shaped floor plan and a straight façade, it is 16.5m long and 8.1m maximum width. The entrance is very impressive being three huge blocks of stone, it leads to an internal corridor 2.7m long giving access to the upper and lower chambers. The lower chamber is entered through a perforated slab of stone and is 6.8m by 2.5m with a similar height. The upper chamber has lost its roof which was probably constructed from large horizontal slabs of stone similar to that of the lower chamber. Within the lower chamber were found various forms of pottery, parts of a necklace and pieces of bronze.

Torralba d'en Salort

Camí Vell de Torralba
Restricted access

Situated to the south of the Me-1, turn left at the second major junction at Alaior, it is signposted.

This prehistoric village covers quite a large area but is worth visiting because it has some very well-preserved elements, the highlight being the taula and its enclosure. The taula is one of the largest on the island at nearly 5m high and 2.5m wide constructed from two smoothed blocks in perfect balance. To the left of the taula is the altar where a small bronze statue of a bull with two terracotta figures were found, possibly representing the fertility goddess Demeter. Other evidence from excavations includes sacrificed sheep, goats and pigs (finds are in the Museum of Menorca). The sacred enclosure which surrounds the taula is in extremely good condition with massive upright blocks forming part of the horseshoe-shaped walls.

Figure 11.9. Torralba d'en Salort

There are also two talayots, the larger and better preserved one is on a small hill to reinforce the idea that one of the functions of these was as lookout towers. There is also a very well-preserved hypostyle room (with columns), the foundations of houses, some underground rooms and a section of the surrounding cyclopean wall. Evidence suggests that the village was occupied from about 1,000 BC until Roman times. A 17th century house and chapel show that later occupation also took place here.

Torre d'en Galmés

Camí de sa Camí
Restricted access

South of the Me-1, take the third major junction at Alaior (from the east) towards Son Bou, signposted to the site. There is a car park.

This is another large prehistoric village situated on a low hill, at over 6ha it is one of the largest on the island, and there is a lot to see. There are three talayots which are relatively well preserved from the top of which are good views all the way to the south coast. These also provided views of several nearby contemporary villages. The open area between the talayots could have been a public meeting place. Evidence here starts from about 1,400 BC.

One of the highlights of this site are the houses in the southeastern area, two of which have been recently excavated by the Museum of Menorca where many of the finds are on display. One of the houses seems to have been abandoned in a hurry and a whole range of artefacts including very nice pottery and tools were

Figure 11.10. A display board at Torre d'en Galmés

Figure 11.11. Torre d'en Galmés

left on the floor. The houses are circular with rooms arranged around a central courtyard where the hearth and water container are located. One of the houses has a connected underground storage room. There is also a well-preserved hypostyle room with columns and roof slabs. Some of the houses were modified by the Romans to have more rectangular shaped rooms built from smaller stones. There was also some Islamic occupation of the site, and alteration of buildings, thought to be by Muslims fleeing the Reconquista of the mainland.

The sacred enclosure with a taula is also very well preserved showing many of the large upright stones forming the horseshoe-shaped wall. One unusual feature found towards the south of this site is the very sophisticated water management system. A series of underground chambers were used to store water with channels connecting these cisterns, one is a re-used pre-talayotic tomb dating to *c.* 1,400 BC. The depressions in the bedrock are thought to have been filled with pebbles to form a water filtering system.

Torre Sant Agustí

Camí de Sant Agustí Nou
Unrestricted access

Take the Me-18 from the Me-1 at Es Mercadal, about 1.5km south of Es Migjorn Gran turn right onto the Camí de Sant Agustí Nou, the site is about 1km on the right. This is a private estate but access is allowed.

This village has two talayots, the largest of which is very special and interesting. It is of the usual massive dry-stone walling construction but has a doorway which leads via a corridor to a circular internal chamber with a high ceiling

Figure 11.12. The eastern Talayot at Torre Sant Agustí

supported by stone columns. This is stone built but has original wooden beams still in place. Analysis has shown these to be wild olive wood and they have been radiocarbon dated to the 9th century BC. The remains of a large rectangular building are attached to the talayot, similar to the site of Cornia Nou (above) where there was evidence for large-scale food production and storage.

The second talayot, to the east, is also interesting showing concentric rings of construction. Elsewhere on the site are the remains of at least seven houses and possible taula enclosures none of which are very well preserved.

Torre Trencada

Camí Torre Trancadeta
Unrestricted access

About 6km east of Ciutadella the site is signposted south of the Me-1 along the Camí Binigarba, turn left after 1km then after 2km there is a car park for the site.

This is a nice, peaceful shaded site with several interesting features. The highlight of this site is the taula which is extremely well preserved and unusual in having an extra supporting upright. The taula sanctuary is not well preserved although parts of its wall can be seen incorporated into a modern wall. There is also a well-preserved hypostyle room which may have been used to collect rainwater making it a kind of cistern.

Figure 11.13. Torre Trencada

Like many talayotic villages this one was used through the Roman and Islamic periods. Here there are also a series of rock-cut graves which are probably medieval. Not far from these is a relatively modern system for collecting rainwater channelling it into underground reservoirs, two of which may have been prehistoric burial chambers.

Torrellafuda

Son Camps
Unrestricted access

South of the Me-1, signposted along Son Camps after about 88m there is a car park, walk to the site opposite. This site is not well preserved and wouldn't rank high on our list of must sees although it is a peaceful place to spend a short time.

Figure 11.14. The enclosing wall of Torrellafuda

Before you reach the talayot there are some burial chambers. Behind the talayot there is a taula enclosure with a complete taula, there are also some houses. The highlight of this site is probably the remains of the massive stone wall that enclosed the original village, it is rubble filled and has two entrances. The wall has been modified in more recent times but gives a good feel for its original size (see also Son Catlar below).

Naveta des Tudons

Restricted access

Located on the Me-1, 4km outside Ciutadella. Park and walk to the site which is surrounded by a modern wall.

This remarkable structure is the most visited tourist attraction on Menorca and it is easy to see why. It is the largest and best preserved of several dozen navetas on the island (and on Mallorca), the construction resembling a massive upside-down stone boat hull (nave in Spanish) in plan with the entrance façade being the stern and the apse shaped rear the prow. Originally it would probably have been about 6m high, today it is about 5m and 14.5m long and 6.5m wide. It was excavated in 1959/60 and partially restored. It is not possible to go inside the naveta.

The walls consist of huge blocks of dressed limestone which are corbelled towards the top and sit on a foundation layer of even bigger blocks. In the façade is a narrow entrance which originally would have been closed by a slab.

Figure 11.15. Naveta des Tudons

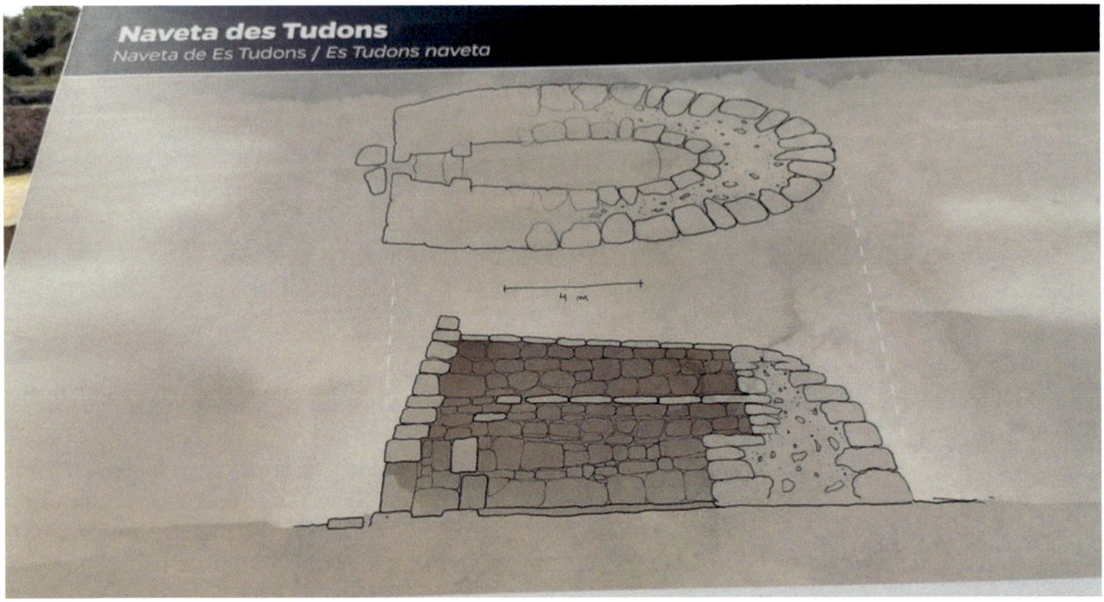

Figure 11.16. A display board at Naveta des Tudons

This leads to a short passage which enters into an antechamber then another short passage into the main chamber which is 7.5m by 2,45m. The ceiling is made from massive stone slabs about 2.25m above the floor. Accessible from this chamber is an upper chamber, slightly smaller at 7.1m by 1.9m and 0.85m high, again with a slabbed ceiling.

Navetas are collective burial chambers and this one has provided good evidence for how they would have functioned. The upper chamber was probably used for the drying of corpses, when disarticulated the individual bones were moved to the lower chamber and deposited with grave goods. Excavation here revealed the remains of over 100 individuals, one with a trepanned skull, buried with a range of artefacts including bronze bracelets, bone and ceramic buttons and pottery (displayed in the Museum of Menorca). Radiocarbon dates from here and other Menorcan navetas show a period of use from about 1,130 BC to 820 BC although this could be partially later re-use of monuments constructed earlier.

Figure 11.17. Looking into the entrance of Naveta des Tudons

Figure 11.18. Son Catlar

Son Catlar

Camí de San Saura
Restricted access

From the Rc-2 on the southern outskirts of Ciutadella take the Camí de Sant Joan de Missa, after 4km turn right to San Saura, the site is after 3km with a car park.

This is the largest talayotic site on the island at over 6ha and there is plenty to see as indicated on an information board with different walking routes. There are other information boards in English. The magnificent highlight of this site is the massive cyclopean wall that surrounds the village. It is constructed of large stones, is 2m wide and at nearly 1km in length completely surrounds the site. Other villages on the island have short lengths of surrounding wall but this one is by far the best. At points along the wall are defensive bastions and at the northern side is a well-preserved entrance with a truly massive lintel stone. It is worth walking around the outside of the wall.

The interior of the site is not as well preserved as some others but is still worth exploring, it includes five talayots, a taula enclosure with a broken taula and some houses.

Necropolis Cala Morell

Carrer Lira
Unrestricted access

On the coast about 12km north of Ciutadella. From the Rc-1 on the northern outskirts of Ciutadella follow the signs for Cala Morell. At the beginnings of the residential area turn left and the car park is on the right.

Figure 11.19. Necropolis Cala Morell

This is a very well laid out site with good information boards in English. Here are fourteen caves situated in a gully that feeds into the cove. Some of them are extremely well preserved and show interior columns (some with capitals), windows and shaped rooms as well as exterior carved façades.

The earliest tombs date to around 1,600 BC and are two small artificial caves with an entrance of stones and pottery found inside as grave goods. During the Iron Age, about 600 BC, the necropolis was expanded with large caves constructed for collective burial. The dead and their grave goods were covered with quicklime. Some of the tombs have places at the door where food was left in pots for use by the dead in the afterlife. The necropolis was in use until the 2nd century AD. One of the highlights is tomb number 4 which has a carved façade showing Etruscan and Punic architectural traits indicating the wide trading links across the Mediterranean. At places carved into the cliff wall are small niches thought to be for burial urns of children.

Index